Special thanks to:

Fantrax: I used Fantrax throughout the process of writing and publishing this book. Their league commissioner services are the best and most customizable on the market. There are a wide range of features that aren't available anywhere else. You can migrate any of your current leagues there without issue, keeping all current rules in place. The amount of time commissioners can save by switching to Fantrax is staggering.

RotoExperts, Pro Football Focus, FF Today, Fifth Down Blog, and Fantasy Football Starters: All leaders in terms of providing unique, useful fantasy content, these sites allowed me to publish various articles prior to, during, and after the process of writing *Fantasy Football for Smart People*.

Fantasy Football Calculator, FJ Fantasy, and Terez Owens: All provided prizes and supported my marketing efforts

Jessica: For all your support and love, I'm very grateful.

Table of Contents

Chapter 1: *The Most In-Depth Introduction You'll Ever Read*

This is an introduction, but I dive right into complex draft strategy, explaining how position scarcity, consistency, game theory, and league requirements are the four pillars of fantasy football draft strategy.

- How to use scarcity at a position to acquire maximum value
- How to use your opponents' beliefs to get the best players
- Why predictability is more important than projected points

Chapter 2: *Why Week-to-Week Consistency is (Almost) Worthless*

An explanation of why weekly projections are of little value, why season-to-season consistency is invaluable, and how to implement risk

- Why you should start a nearly identical lineup each week
- How to create tiered rankings that implement players' risk
- When and how to take gambles during your draft

Chapter 3: *Season-to-Season Consistency: Why It Matters and How to Use it*

The strength of correlation of fantasy football statistics from one year to the next

- How stats like rushing, receiving, and passing yards/touchdowns translate from one season to another
- Why defenses and kickers are almost entirely unpredictable
- Why a quarterback or top-tier running back should be your first-round selection
- Why tight ends are the most consistent players in fantasy football

Chapter 4: *Tier-ing Up: How to Create Basic Projections and Tiered Rankings*

Basic projection philosophy, including how to use consistency, risk, and average draft position to create rankings

- A basic formula to create projections
- How to make tiers in your rankings
- Why you should almost never take the best player available on your board (for real)
- Why drafting near the end of a round is advantageous

Chapter 5: *More on Position Scarcity*

A short chapter on scarcity and VORP draft strategy

- Why Aaron Rodgers and Rob Gronkowski might be the perfect 1-2 combination in 2012
- Why you can grab quality wide receivers late

Chapter 6: *Identifying Value: Regression, Randomness, and Running Backs*

Using stats to identify breakout players and dispel fantasy football "trusisms"

- How to identify undervalued players
- Why running backs with lots of carries aren't *really* being overworked or overvalued
- How to predict running backs' yards-per-carry

Chapter 7: *Getting Bullish: What the Stock Market Can Teach Us About Fantasy Football*

How fantasy football is incredibly similar to the stock market (and what we can learn from the latter)

- Why a player's value can be different for different teams
- How to "buy low" and "sell high" during your draft
- How to utilize public perception
- Why your focus shouldn't be securing the most projected points with each pick, but rather "losing" the least

Chapter 8: *The Ultimate Draft Plan: From Projections to Selections*

Creating an overarching draft plan to dominate your draft

- Specific formulas to project player stats
- How to factor league requirements into your rankings
- Sample breakdowns of Matt Ryan and Steve Smith
- How to create player power ratings and turn them into the ultimate big board

Chapter 9: *Don't Mock Me: Oh, now wait. Go ahead.*

Taking you through three mock drafts I completed in May

- Notes on all 60 draft picks
- Tips on strategy from specific draft slots

Chapter 1: Fantasy Football for Smart People: How to Dominate Your Draft

The Most In-Depth Introduction You'll Ever Read

Note: These first few pages are a brief introduction to a rather complex draft strategy. So why start with it? You can't build a house without a frame, and the concepts mentioned in this intro will be the foundation of the rest of my analysis. If you struggle to fully grasp all of the ideas mentioned in the densely-packed first few pages, fear not, as more detailed and all-encompassing breakdowns will follow in subsequent sections.

Fantasy football draft strategy can be paradoxical in that the most effective way to garner the maximum projected points for your team does *not* necessarily involve selecting the players who will score the most points. Wait, huh? How can you maximize projected points without drafting the players who will, you know, score the most points?

The Major Players: Starting Lineup Requirements and Position Scarcity

The reason temporarily bypassing maximum "value" can be beneficial deals with position scarcity and starting lineup requirements. Let's starts with the latter. In fantasy football, you are obviously required to start a specific number of players at different positions. If you could simply start your highest-scoring players, quarterbacks would fill the first few rounds of drafts.

Since fantasy football requires you to start players at positions that naturally score fewer points than other positions (think kickers), at some point in your draft, it is necessary to bypass a high-scoring position for a lower-scoring one. The best fantasy football owners understand how to balance that delicate task.

Of course, the "best" time to take a quarterback, or a running back, or any other position changes based on a number of factors, including the season, your league rules, your previous draft picks, and so on. One of the factors that can help us determine which position to take at each spot is standard deviation. Standard deviation is the measure of diversity in a group of statistics; the greater the range of measurements from the average, the greater the deviation.

For fantasy football owners, standard deviation means identifying "outliers" within each position. For example, assume the top quarterback in the NFL scored around 1,000 fantasy points each season. Gotta grab him in the first round, right? Not necessarily, even if you know with 100% confidence which player will be the top quarterback in such a hypothetical league. If quarterbacks 2-12 scored about 990 points each year, the value of the top quarterback is miniscule. In that example, there is no outlier; the top signal-caller's projected total is almost identical to the 11 quarterbacks behind him.

Whereas standard deviation relates to the diversity of points among players at a particular position, position scarcity is a comparison of diversity *among* positions. The two are very similar, but in essence position scarcity is a tool that incorporates standard deviation, and one that can greatly enhance your ability to draft efficiently. All other things equal, it is prudent to select players who are the "scarcest" at their position, regardless of the particular position they play or their projected points. Position scarcity allows you to decide which position to draft, and standard deviation helps identify the best player at that position.

So we know starting lineup requirements necessitate the selection of "non-optimal" players at certain spots, and we know both standard deviation and its cousin position scarcity can aid us in picking the right players at the right spots.

This, in a nutshell, is what VORP (Value Over Replacement Player) is all about. Most frequently used in baseball statistics, I've broadened the definition of the term a bit as it relates to fantasy football draft strategy. For our purposes, a 'replacement player' is the "next best" player at a specific position who could be drafted in subsequent rounds if the current top-rated player is bypassed. Let's use an example.

Suppose you are in the fifth round of your draft and you are deciding between drafting a tight end or selecting a wide receiver. The top-rated tight end on your board is projected to score 180 points, but if you bypass him he will almost certain be taken. The next best tight end you could land in round six is projected to score 160 points. Meanwhile, your top-ranked receiver is projected to score 220 points, with the next best at the position who you could draft in the sixth round projected at 210 points.

And the correct choice is. . .the tight end. Despite being projected to score fewer points than the wide receivers, your top tight end is 20 points ahead of the next best. If you take him and grab the second-ranked receiver in the sixth round, you are sitting pretty at 390 projected points. If you bypass the top tight end for the "best player available" in the wide receiver, you will be left with a total of 380 projected points. The top tight end has a greater standard deviation compared to others at his position, meaning he is scarcer.

But that's not the end of the story.

Game Theory: A Brief Aside

Fantasy football is a game of competing decision-makers, i.e. others minds are involved. Almost all aspects of the game are zero-sum, meaning when one owner gains, another loses. It is really a complex game of rock-paper-scissors. As such, we can and should use game theory as a mode of decision-making.

Game theory is a strategic decision-making process that applies to zero-sum games, and wherein the beliefs of others affect your decisions. It is worth noting NFL play-calling is all about game theory; run when they expect you to pass, and vice versa. While game theory is an umbrella term that can apply to a plethora of processes, I've always liked to think of it as acting one step ahead of your opponents.

One of the greatest examples of game theory implementation I have ever uncovered was an at-bat in the 1990s between Padres slugger Tony Gwynn and Braves pitcher Greg Maddux. Both ballplayers were among the most intelligent in Major League Baseball at the time, and as a result their battles at the plate were a chess match.

The count was two balls and one strike, and Gwynn knew in this situation Maddux liked to throw a breaking pitch. A lot of hitters might stop right there, looking for a curve. But Gwynn knew Maddux was a smart guy, and he understood Maddux was often a step ahead of hitters. Maddux knew that Gwynn knew that Maddux was likely to throw a breaking ball. So Maddux decided to deliver a heater.

But Gwynn, in all his glory, knew that (and stay with me here) Maddux knew that Gwynn knew that Maddux liked to throw breaking balls in 2-1 counts. So Gwynn looked for what other hitters might deem the least likely pitch: a fastball. Gwynn's knowledge of Maddux's thoughts about Gwynn helped Gwynn look for the right pitch. And he hit a home run.

This is quintessential game theory, and its implementation into both the NFL and fantasy football can significantly enhance win probability. So when NFL coaches claim they are concerned only with their game plan and aren't focused on what the opponent will try to do, they are either lying, or soon to be coaching high school football.

Game Theory's Value in Fantasy Football

A few years ago, I was discussing an upcoming fantasy draft with my dad (who is part of my dynasty league and was new to the game that year). He mentioned he was thinking of taking Bears running back Matt Forte with the second overall selection. At that time, Forte wasn't going in the first few rounds of drafts (he was ranked No. 43 overall by ESPN that year).

Naturally, I asked him why he would draft Forte so high. "Because he's going to score the second-most points," he quickly replied.

Seems straightforward enough, and if we use a traditional draft strategy (and even a complex one such as VORP), Forte might be the guy to whom the numbers lead. If my dad had him ranked far ahead of the third option such that Forte's value made him an outlier among running backs, conventional fantasy football draft strategy says to draft him.

But we all know that isn't right. You don't win championships by selecting fourth-round projected players in the top two picks, even if you think they will lead the league in points. So it's quite obvious we need to implement game theory into our draft strategies, even if it is in the form of a quick comparison to consensus rankings. The beliefs of the competition *must* affect our decisions. The extent to which we can utilize game theory and the methodology we employ to do so will be the subject of later analysis.

You're So Predictable

There's a final component of complex fantasy football draft strategy, and it is two-pronged. Predictability in fantasy football is absolutely vital to draft success, and it is one of the most overlooked aspects of the process. By predictability, I mean the ability to correctly assess the consistency inherent to particular positions, as well as each player within a position.

Let's take an example. Suppose the top defense in fantasy football scores an obscene amount of points in a given year (we'll again say 1,000), and all other defenses are very far behind. Securing the No. 1 defense in this hypothetical scenario obviously holds tremendous value. Do so, and you basically win the league.

Also note a draft strategy that combines VORP and game theory would lead to the hypothetical selection of your top-rated defense at every draft spot. If you project the Steelers to score 1,000 points and every other team defense to tally around 200, for example, clearly the Steelers are extremely "scarce." Further, if every other owner has similar projections, game theory would advocate selecting Pittsburgh's D with the No. 1 overall pick.

So why might this be an obviously boneheaded move? Because if there is very little predictability within team defenses from year to year, the early selection of one is illogical. As long as there is a limit to the number of defenses you can draft, the scarcity of the top defense has zero value to an owner if it is impossible to predict *which* defense will score those 1,000 points. With no predictive ability, you would be just as likely to draft the top defense in the last round as the first.

As fantasy owners, we want to minimize the luck that is inherent to the game. The early selection of a position whose year-to-year rankings are basically as predictable as a roulette wheel increases the luck needed to win.

Interestingly, the lack of predictability among team defenses in my hypothetical scenario is not far from reality. Actually, there is just about no predictive ability within the position. Defenses that finished high in the fantasy rankings in a given year are no more likely to do so the following year than the bottom dwellers from the previous season.

Predictability Among Players

The ability to predict the final rankings within a given position is a matter of consistency; how consistent are top fantasy performers at particular positions? I will of course analyze this topic more, but another form of predictability and consistency with which we need to concern ourselves is that among individual players.

We all know certain players carry more risk than others heading into a football season. Whether it is due to poor character or an injury in the previous season, there are players we label as "high risk/high reward," and the risk we associate with them has huge implications on our ability to predict their future performance.

In 2011, I had Chris Johnson projected to score the most fantasy points among all running backs, ahead of Adrian Peterson, Ray Rice, and Arian Foster. But I had CJ2K ranked behind all of those players because the risk surrounding Johnson's contract situation and potential holdout made the ability to predict his 2011 performance quite volatile. The greater the ability to predict a player's performance, the more weight that can be given to his projections.

Now, there are formulas I use to assess risk/reward (read on, grasshopper), and there are certainly times when gambling on a high-risk player is prudent. The entire fantasy draft process is a collection of calculated gambles, and with the right use of statistics, you can tilt the scales in your favor.

What To Anticipate

As you read on, try to remember the overarching concepts of VORP, game theory, and predictability that lie at the core of draft strategy. With these notions in mind, I will take you through a more in-depth analysis of each idea, hitting on a variety of subcategories in the process. Among the topics I will discuss are:

- Why week-to-week consistency is almost worthless

- Why you should wait until the last two rounds for a defense and kicker

- The myth of the "overworked" running back

- Why tight end is the most predictable position

- Why fantasy football is a stock market

- The value of pairing a receiver with his quarterback

- How to create power rating systems based on projections, then tiered-rankings based on your power ratings

- How regression can be exploited

- Why quarterback rushing yards are valuable

- Why quarterback/tight end might be the best 1-2 punch in 2012

- How to predict yards-per-carry (and a lot of other stats)

- How to incorporate consensus rankings into your board

- Why you should perform mock drafts

- A whole lot more

A lot of the material in this book will be complex, and you will certainly develop questions and opinions along the way. I love to discuss fantasy football, so please feel free to e-mail at jonathan@thedctimes.com if you find something unclear or wish to point out the merits of an opposing view.

Also note the format of the book is not necessarily sequential. Some sections build upon the material in others, but the book is really synonymous to a collection of short stories. As such, don't be alarmed if you don't completely grasp every term in each section. If the idea is an essential one, I will address it further. At the end of the book, it is my hope you will develop a more comprehensive understanding of fantasy football strategies.

Finally, "The Bottom Line" categories at the end of each section should help you quickly digest the most pressing information. They are simplified, pragmatic versions of the more complex material, and they provide tips on how to transfer the analysis into practical applications for your team.

Enjoy, and best of luck in the 2012 fantasy football season!

Chapter 2: Why Week-to-Week Consistency is (Almost) Worthless

One of the largest misconceptions among fantasy football owners is the importance of intensely analyzing weekly matchups to select a starting lineup. It is all too easy to outsmart yourself and wind up starting your fourth receiver over your top back in a flex spot because the receiver tore apart the opposing cornerback in their last matchup.

Start Your Studs

In reality, the success players see in individual games is far more strongly correlated with opportunity than opponent. Yes, there are weekly random fluctuations wherein under-the-radar rookie wide receivers go for 90 yards and a touchdown or your stud running back totals just 30 yards and goes catch-less, but the majority of the time, **fantasy football lineup decisions aren't brain surgery: start your studs.**

There are really only a few times when you even need to make a decision regarding who to start, in my view:

- Extreme circumstances

If your top receiver is visiting Revis Island this week or just lost his starting quarterback, by all means, think about sitting him. Similarly, a kicker playing in 40 mph winds is a no-go.

- Flex spots

In "close calls," such as whether to start a third running back or a fourth wide receiver in your flex spot, some stat analysis and a little research can help.

- Defenses

While year-to-year defensive play is almost totally random, you can alter your starting defense each week based on the opponent. Fumbles and defensive/special teams touchdowns are random, but yards against (to an extent) and, particularly, interceptions have some predictive value. It is okay to sit the top defense if you have a mediocre one playing a squad with a rookie quarterback and an injured left tackle. This is a book on how to dominate your draft, but in-season moves like those above have an impact on which players you should select. . .

Consistency's Place in Fantasy Football

Related to this idea is the notion of week-to-week consistency. Do a search for 'fantasy football consistency' and, other than one of my articles that bashes the importance of week-to-week consistency, you'll find all sorts of consistency ratings and player rankings based on it. It's really a sham, because if you start your top players at each position each week, regardless of their volatility, the consistency is irrelevant.

But what about searching for consistency in drafts? Should you target players that possess week-to-week consistency? Well, not really, because true week-to-week consistency might not even exist. Numerous studies have shown the perception of players' weekly consistency to be an illusion based on past performance. The problem with past performance, in terms of weekly consistency, is that it has very little predictive value. Put another way, players who have performed consistently on a week-to-week basis in the past are no more likely to do so in the future than a player who hasn't been consistent.

Note that I am not only talking about performing consistently *well* each week; if a player scores between just three and five points each and every week, that's consistency too. Regardless of the points scored, though, it appears we are justified in saying "consistency schmasistency."

Consistency and Risk: Is a Risky Team Bad?

While selecting specific individual players to start each week won't necessarily increase a team's volatility, pairing particular players together can do the trick. Specifically, pairing a quarterback and a wide receiver (or tight end) that are on the same NFL team inherently increases risk, as the success of the latter is based on the former.

Increasing risk can't be a good thing, can it? For bad teams, yes. If your team is consistently scoring below the league average in points, do everything you can to increase its volatility. If the mean point total in your league is 100 and you average just 75, consistently scoring 75 points will rarely net you a win. If you greatly enhance the inherent "risk" associated with your team and score 130 points from time to time, you'll at least gather a handful of victories.

Similarly, good teams should limit risk as much as possible. This can be accomplished by avoiding such quarterback and pass-catcher pairings, or by starting a pass-catcher of your opponent's stud quarterback. In the latter scenario, you naturally decrease your odds of losing by potentially limiting the effect of an "outlier" breakout game for your opponent's quarterback. If the quarterback goes off, chances are the receiver will as well.

One notable exception, and a strategy I like to employ at times, is pairing your backup quarterback with one of your top receivers. If you need to regularly start your backup quarterback, chances are your team isn't doing so hot. In that scenario, you will benefit from the increased upside provided by a quarterback-receiver combination.

Seasonal Consistency: Why It's Crucial
There's quite a difference between week-to-week consistency and consistency over seasons, and the latter is vital to your success as an owner. As I stated earlier, draft strategies are worthless without predictability, and predictions are impossible without year-to-year consistency; otherwise, drafts would be a crapshoot.

Whereas in-season risk can effectively be ignored, the risk associated with a particular player entering the season is crucial to projections.

Objectivity in Fantasy Land?
Nearly all "objective" measures in life have some sort of subjective aspect to them, and the same is true of fantasy football projections. We can create formulas to determine which players to select at each spot, and in some sense this is objective analysis. But the formulas are governed by subjective input, i.e. projections, risk analysis, and so on.

Nonetheless, once we determine the appropriate value of subjective statistics such as projected points and inherent risk, we can create objective formulas to interpret the results.

In the intro, I briefly discussed downgrading Chris Johnson to No. 4 on my running back board due to the risk surrounding his playing status, despite the fact that I had him projected to score the most points. One of the major reasons I did this is because early-round picks should be on "can't-miss" players. Every potential first-round pick naturally has a high ceiling, so it is prudent to minimize downside early. The middle and late rounds are the best times to take risks.

In my Johnson example, the risk surrounding the Titans running back in 2011 came from uncertainty. How will Johnson's holdout affect his play? Will a new offensive coordinator utilize Johnson appropriately? Did Johnson's long scampers the season before hint he was due for a natural regression toward the mean?

These questions create uncertainty in the minds of owners, and that uncertainty is represented as risk. It is also a type of risk that is difficult to quantify, and I'm not sure it is even possible to place an objective measure on it. What are the chances a holdout, new coordinator, and natural regression affect Johnson's 2011 play? We can estimate those numbers, but we don't really know.

Personally, I created a formula to determine how often I thought Johnson would perform below particular baselines, ranking him behind those backs that ranked ahead of him at those points more frequently. Scroll ahead to "The Ultimate Draft Plan: From Projections to Selections" for more detailed analysis on how to project running back points and use year-to-year consistency in your rankings.

How to Use Consistency Within Tiers
Of course, implementing consistency doesn't need to be so complex. If you sort players at each position into tiers, as I recommend, you can easily rank the players in each tier inversely accordingly to the risk surrounding them. This way, you garner the benefits of employing consistency into your rankings without drastically altering the order.

For example, assume you have developed the following projections and risk analysis for 2012:

Drew Brees – 400 points Risk: 6/10
Aaron Rodgers – 395 points Risk: 1/10
Peyton Manning – 390 points Risk: 9/10
Tom Brady – 385 points Risk: 3/10
Cam Newton – 360 points Risk: 8/10
Matthew Stafford – 355 points Risk: 5/10
Tony Romo – 350 points Risk: 3/10

In this hypothetical example, it is pretty easy to see we should place Rodgers, Brees, Brady, and Manning into Tier 1. With the precipitous drop in points following Manning, you would define Tier 2 to include Newton, Stafford, and Romo.

Now, we simply need to alter the rankings to accommodate our risk analysis. Instead of ranking Manning last overall because he holds a ton of risk entering the 2012 campaign, however, he simply falls to last in his tier. After factoring risk into our projections, our final rankings look like this:

Tier 1
Aaron Rodgers
Tom Brady
Drew Brees
Peyton Manning

Tier 2
Tony Romo
Matthew Stafford
Cam Newton

Quick and easy.

How to Recognize True Risk

You may have noticed I have used the terms 'risk' and 'consistency' interchangeably, and that is because, for fantasy football owners, risk is simply a measure of a player's ability to perform consistently from year to year, i.e. how sure can we be a player's future success will be a reflection of past performance? A lot of factors go into determining risk, but there are times when situations appear riskier than reality.

One such example is from the 2010 season, when Steelers quarterback Ben Roethlisberger was suspended four games. For a lot of fantasy owners, that spelled his fantasy death. Roethlisberger fell way too far in fantasy drafts, with some owners even taking him off their boards.

A few hard-working fantasy owners even calculated Roethlisberger's new projected points based on a 12-game season, then ranked him accordingly. This sort of analysis is flawed, however, as it assumes Roethlisberger's presence in a fantasy lineup cannot be replaced.

In reality, those who drafted Roethlisberger to be their starting quarterback for the last 12 games of the season needed to start a replacement player for the first four. The projections for Roethlisberger should actually include the projected points of a replacement quarterback for the first four games of the season.

Let's look at an example. Assume you projected Roethlisberger to score 250 points in 12 games. When deciding between Roethlisberger and a quarterback (who we'll call Player X) who is projected to score 280 points, most naïve owners would select the latter player. More points, less risk, right?

Not really. See, there wasn't "true" risk surrounding Roethlisberger in 2010. It wasn't ideal to draft a quarterback who would net zero points over the first quarter of the season, but Roethlisberger was still himself. Unless you thought he was going to get arrested again, you knew you would be getting a low-end QB1 over the fantasy season's final 11 games.

If you had gone with Player X, you would have received 18.7 points per game over his 15 fantasy starts (assuming he doesn't play in Week 17, and of course during his bye week). Meanwhile, Roethlisberger's 250 points over 11 games equates to 22.7 points per contest. Even if we assume a replacement quarterback would average just 10 points over the season's initial four games, that would still result in an average of 19.3 points for Roethlisberger and the replacement quarterback.

The moral of the story is to recognize the difference between true risk versus perceived risk, as well as when it is smart to take on that risk. It is can be costly to fold a full house, but it is debilitating to bet the house on it and lose.

The Bottom Line
- Start your studs every week, except in rare circumstances.

- Rotate defenses based on matchup.

- Ignore the "value" of week-to-week consistency.

- Season-to-season consistency matters.

- Risk is a measure of consistency. You can factor it into your rankings by re-arranging players within tiers according to risk.

- Know when to gamble. Early in the draft is not the time, but the middle and late rounds should be all about upside.

Chapter 3: Season-to-Season Consistency: Why It Matters and How to Use it

I previously discussed the irrelevancy of weekly consistency, arguing that the only aspect of consistency that should matter to fantasy owners is seasonal. The value of this consistency varies based on the current state of your team (remember, poor teams should look to increase volatility), but understanding which players are valuable each year and which players are high risk/high reward is important for fantasy owners.

Prior to assessing the volatility and consistency of any individual players, it is useful if we understand their position as a whole. That is, knowing the volatility of an entire position can help us better assess the individuals within that spot. All other things equal, we want to take players whose play is consistent, and thus predictable.

Defenses

Since I discussed the volatility of defenses in my introduction, I will start with this position. Remember, I argued that the projected points for team defenses are basically worthless because top defenses from one season are no more likely to score a lot of points the following year than defenses that were bottom-dwellers. The volatility of the position makes it unpredictable, and thus less valuable to fantasy owners.

Let's take a look at the numbers. The following charts are courtesy of my friend Brian Burke at Advanced NFL Stats, and they are the collection of nearly a decade of data.

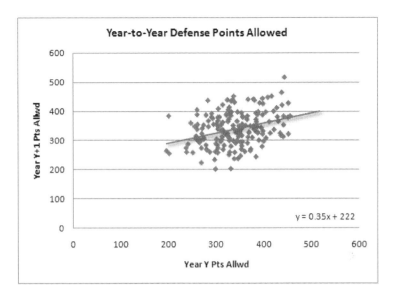

I chose defensive points allowed because this is actually the least volatile defensive statistic for fantasy owners. You can see the correlation between points allowed in year Y and year Y+1 is still very weak at 0.35.

Even so, sacks, yards, takeaways, and special teams points are all far less predictable than points allowed. Plus, the majority of defensive fantasy points tend to come from sacks, takeaways and touchdowns. All are inherently unstable, showing why drafting a defense early is a risky proposition. In case you are wondering, sacks are the next most predictable defensive statistic, but their predictive ability is almost inconsequential.

Kickers

I love to debunk fantasy football "truisms," but the old adage that you should wait until the last round to draft a kicker is here to stay.

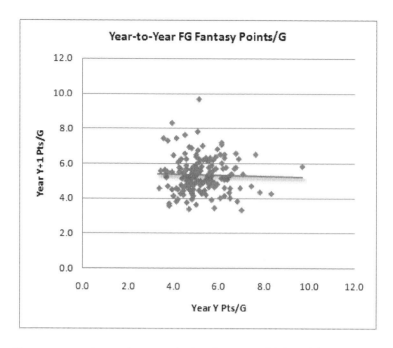

You can see above the correlation between kickers' fantasy points in Year Y and Year Y+1 is actually negative (that is, there is absolutely no meaningful way to predict how many fantasy points a kicker will score). Although extra points are somewhat predictable, the instability of field goal totals makes predicting kicker points a total guessing game. There is simply no way to determine how many times a kicker's team will get into field goal position, how many of those will be "chip shots," and so on.

Running Backs
For years, running backs dominated the first few rounds of fantasy drafts. That trend has slowed down considerably in the last few years, with running backs selected more than any other position in the first round, but not the next few rounds.

One reason for this is because running back consistency has plummeted. Whereas workhorse backs were in vogue in the 1990s and even for a bit post-2000, today's NFL is all about a committee approach. As such, the value of the running back spot, as a whole, has deteriorated.

A funny thing has happened over that time, however. While the overall value of running backs has decreased, the worth of the top backs that still possess some sort of "workhorse" characteristics (think Adrian Peterson, Ray Rice, Chris Johnson, Arian Foster, etc.) has soared. In a league in which only a handful of players are "the guy" in their backfield, acquiring a stud running back has remained a priority for fantasy owners.

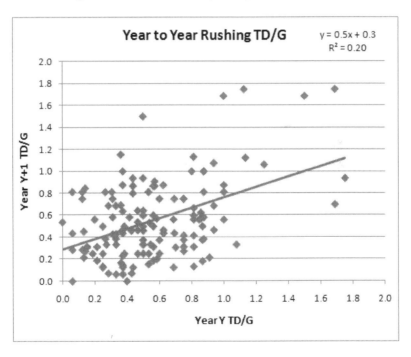

You can see this idea reflected in the charts above and below. There is a fairly strong year-to-year correlation for rushing touchdowns in particular, but that is influenced heavily by the top scorers.

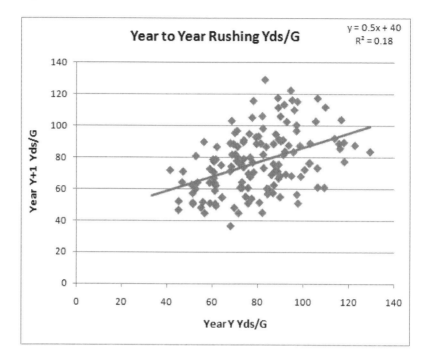

Also note the difference in fantasy points scored in each category. The difference between the top rusher (130 yards per game) and a replacement rusher (90 yards per game) is just four points per contest. On the other hand, the difference between the top scorer (1.6 touchdowns per game) and a replacement scorer (0.6 touchdowns per game) is a full six points.

Since the standard deviation among running back touchdowns is greater than that for yards, the outliers we see in the touchdown plot are even more valuable than they first appear. This is due to the surprising strength of correlation (0.5) for running back touchdowns in year Y and year Y+1.

Overall, the correlation between year-to-year fantasy points for running backs is 0.48. This is very close to the 0.50 correlation for yards and touchdowns, with fluky factors like fumbles dragging down the correlation just a bit.

So what does this all mean? Well, it's still quite important to secure an "outlying" running back, i.e. one of the top-tier guys at the position. If you aren't in position to do so, however, you might as well wait. With the committee approach taken by most teams and the only moderately-strong correlation between mid-tier running back fantasy points from one year to the next, there's no reason to get antsy in the second or third round.

Wide Receivers

When we analyze wide receiver touchdowns and yards, we see a yearly strength of correlation similar to that for running backs.

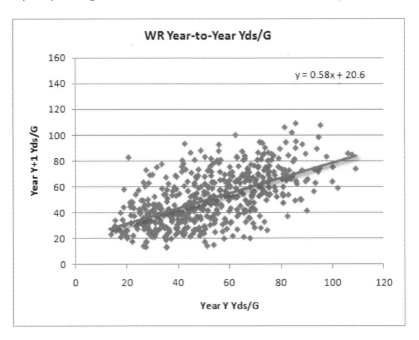

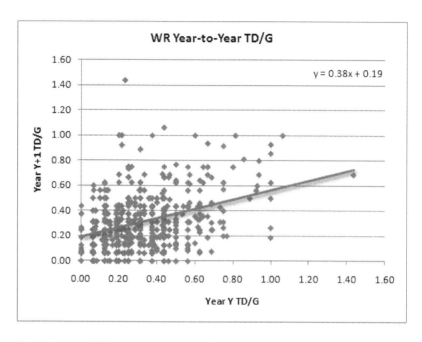

The primary difference between the two positions, as I see it, is the NFL's transition to pass-heavy offenses has made quality receivers more prevalent. The third wide receiver on a team is basically a starter, and in some offenses, he can put up starter-quality fantasy numbers.

The increase in available options and the lack of high consistency at the position means you can find quality wide receiver depth in the middle and even late rounds of the draft, whereas all suitable running back options are pretty much off the board. That's not to say there aren't stud receivers who deserve consideration near the top of the draft. Calvin Johnson is a first-round pick no matter how you slice it.

I think one of the primary reasons wide receivers have such high volatility is the randomness inherent to their position. While all football players are dependent on teammates for their success, it is particularly true for receivers, who need a quality quarterback and a decent offensive line.

Further, wide receivers have a small sample size of plays on which they can score fantasy points. Even No. 1 receiving options play in games where they see just three targets. Although these fluctuations even out a bit over the course of a season, it isn't to the same degree of running backs.

Plus, the success of wide receivers is very dependent on game situations, such as the score and how the defense is playing them. There are only a couple of receivers out there who can regularly beat Cover 2, and because so many similar factors can take a receiver out of a game, their consistency is tarnished (even from season to season). Now throw in an injured quarterback for good measure.

Ultimately, the correlation between wide receiver points in year Y and year Y+1 is about 0.42. Among the top 32 receivers, this number drops to an astonishing 0.35. These numbers suggest receivers are unpredictable across the board, including in the first few rounds.

Quarterbacks

I'm going to talk a whole lot more about the importance of quarterbacks in future sections. In leagues in which you can start two quarterbacks, the position is absolutely critical.

One of the mistakes people make when assessing quarterbacks is placing too much emphasis on touchdowns and interceptions. Let's take a look at the latter stat first.

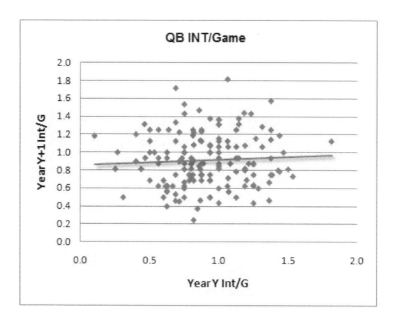

You can see that, at least over the entire quarterback position, there is almost no predictive value for interceptions from year to year. Interceptions are extremely fluky and very likely to regress toward the mean. Projecting any quarterback to throw more than 25 picks is a bad idea.

Touchdown passes are undoubtedly vital to the success of your quarterbacks, but they are not nearly as consistent as passing yards.

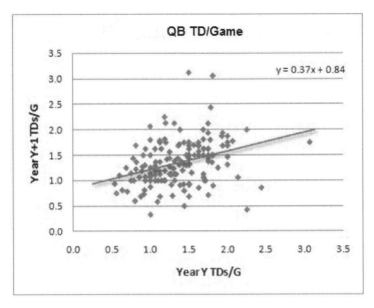

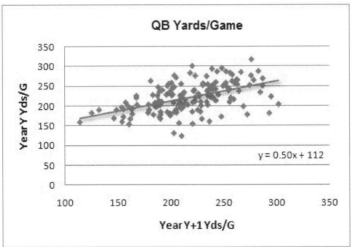

There is a greater slope over a larger data set in the passing yards graph, meaning they are more consistent than touchdowns from season to season. Again, that's not to say passing touchdowns aren't important, but rather that predicting them is more difficult.

Nonetheless, the year-to-year consistency of the league's top signal-callers is astounding. I write with no hesitation that Aaron Rodgers, Tom Brady, and Drew Brees will all be top 10 quarterbacks in 2012, and likely top five. You can't really make a similar claim about any other positions. The consistency of the top-tier quarterbacks is one of the reasons I think selecting one in the first round is a wise move (but more on that later).

As a final note on quarterback consistency, I wanted to point out the most consistent stat in fantasy football from year to year is quarterback rushing yards.

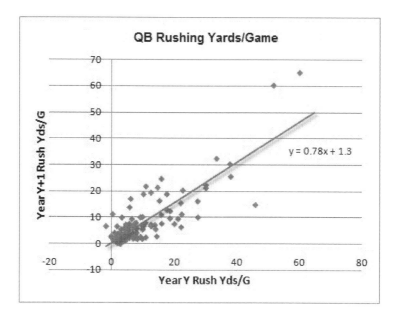

A lot of owners don't factor rushing yards into their quarterback rankings, and this makes the stat very valuable to the fantasy owners who do consider them. "Hidden" stats like quarterback rushing yards are an opportunity for wise owners to gain an advantage. Many write off quarterback rushing yards as inconsequential, but they can be leveraged into an advantage in the same way sports bettors utilize factors that aren't already in the betting line to correctly beat the spread.

Think of it this way. . .although an injured quarterback certainly has a huge effect on the outcome of a game, it does little to affect a bettor's ability to beat the spread, since the injury is already factored into the line. An injured center also affects a game in a substantial way, but this injury is far more valuable to a bettor because it is unlikely to influence the spread.

In a similar way, stats like passing yards are already factored into consensus rankings. By using "hidden" stats like quarterback rushing yards, you can identify true value in a superior manner to your opponents. And you only need to beat your Uncle Bruce, not Vegas.

Nonetheless, the quarterback position is extremely consistent in fantasy football, clocking in at 0.60 correlational strength from year to year.

Tight Ends

The range of opinions regarding the value of tight ends is vast, with some fantasy owners using an early pick on a stud and others waiting until the late rounds to load up on a couple of sleepers with high upside. When assessing tight ends, we need to utilize our knowledge of position scarcity. Let's take a look back to my intro:

> Suppose you are in the fifth round of your draft and you are deciding between drafting a tight end or selecting a wide receiver. The top-rated tight end on your board is projected to score 180 points, but if you bypass him he will almost certain be taken. The next best tight end you could land in round six is projected to score 160

points. Meanwhile, your top-ranked receiver is projected to score 220 points, with the next best at the position who you could draft in the sixth round projected at 210 points.

And the correct choice is. . .the tight end. Despite projected to score fewer points than the wide receivers, your top tight end is 20 points ahead of the next best. If you take him and grab the second-ranked receiver in the sixth round, you are sitting pretty at 390 projected points. If you bypass the top tight end for the "best player available" in the wide receiver, you will be left with a total of 380 projected points. The top tight end has a greater standard deviation compared to others at his position, meaning he is scarcer.

Remember, it is not the total points a player scores that matters, but rather the "worth" of those points when compared to the next best option at his position. This is VORP, and the lack of top-end "replacement" players increases the value of the top-tier tight ends.

On top of all this, tight end statistics appear to be rather consistent from year to year.

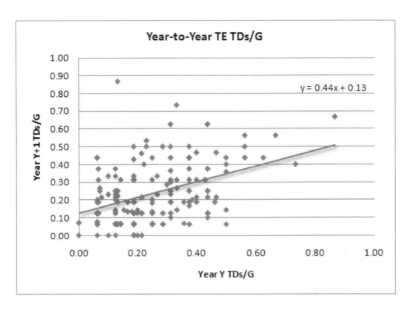

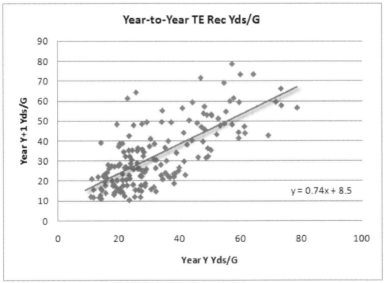

You can see tight end touchdowns are more predictable than any other position except running back, and tight end receiving yards are the second-most consistent stat in all of fantasy football (behind quarterback rushing yards). As a whole, **tight**

ends retain 62% of their performance from year to year, making it the most predictable position in fantasy football.

So what does this mean to you? It means selecting Jimmy Graham or Rob Gronkowski in the early portion of the third round isn't a gamble at all, but rather one of the safest picks you can make in that range.

The Bottom Line

- Defenses and kickers show almost zero consistency from year to year. Wait until the final rounds to draft them (assuming you need to draft them at all).

- Although touchdowns can be susceptible to fluctuations, they are just as consistent for running backs as rushing yards. Running back touchdowns are far more predictable than those for most other positions.

- Try to land an "outlying" running back in the first round. If you can't, don't reach for one in the second and third. The difference between middle-tier backs is small.

- Wide receivers are important, but they aren't as consistent as some other positions. The second or third round is a great time to acquire your No. 1. You can also find quality players at the position in the middle rounds simply because there are more pass-catchers in the NFL today.

- Quarterback interceptions are almost completely random and can effectively be disregarded from projections.

- Quarterback rushing yards are a "hidden" stat and should carry a lot of weight with owners. They also minimize risk.

- Tight end receiving yards are the second-most consistent stat in all of fantasy football. Drafting a top-tier tight end early isn't as risky as people believe.

- First-round selections should be spent on players with high ceilings (low risk). Although quarterbacks as a whole are less predictable than the other skill positions, the top-end quarterbacks consistently finish at the top. In 2012, Aaron Rodgers will be the top player on my board because his VORP is outstanding and he carries as little volatility as any player in the league.

- We can actually use the correlational strength of year-to-year fantasy points among specific positions in our player projections. I will show you how to do that in subsequent sections.

Chapter 4: Tier-ing Up: How to Create Basic Projections and Tiered Rankings

I've talked a bit about player stat projections and their importance in our rankings, but why make projections at all? Why not simply rank players at their respective positions based on last year's final rankings and a few subjective factors?

The most obvious answer is stat projections simply help with our rankings. By projecting a player's yards, touchdowns, and so on, it becomes far easier to determine how he ranks among his peers.

This is particularly true with players whose stats don't necessarily match up with their true value to their football team. Back before Michael Vick went to jail, for example, he was always a player whose fantasy value didn't match up with his perceived value. With the exception of a few stretches of incredible play and even with his rushing prowess, Vick was never really a dominating figure in fantasy football. Despite that, owners continued to overdraft him because we all knew he was valuable to the Atlanta Falcons.

Another reason it is smart to perform stat projections is the ease with which you can then rank and re-rank players based on league scoring. Michael Turner is a solid running back in traditional fantasy formats, but in leagues with point-per-reception scoring, he's basically a third option at the position. Projecting stats and later developing rankings from those projections simplifies the process.

The most important reason we need to make projections, though, ties back in with the idea of VORP. Remember, VORP, or Value Over Replacement Player, suggests we should identify the biggest gap in points between current draft considerations and replacement players at their respective positions who could be drafted later.

The example between wide receivers and tight ends that I used in the tight end section of my analysis of season-to-season consistency is an example of an employment of VORP. In effect, VORP is the temporary bypassing of maximum points for greater overall points down the road. Remember, since fantasy football requires the selection of players from multiple positions, any worthwhile draft strategy must possess an overarching vision; draft strategies like "Best Player Available" are too shortsighted, unnecessarily limiting the projected points you can acquire down the road in favor of more now.

Without projections (or some sort of rating system), VORP draft strategy is impossible. A value system is necessary to decipher the "worth" of a player. We can rank players all day to help us compare players *within* particular positions, but a comparison of players that play different positions is worthless without a rating system.

How to Add Positional Consistency Into Projections

One quick and easy method to implement positional consistency into player ratings is to multiply projected points for a position by the correlational strength of consistency. That is:

$C(P)$, where C is correlational strength and P is projected points

As I stated earlier, these correlations are 0.62 for tight ends, 0.60 for quarterbacks, 0.48 for running backs, and 0.42 for wide receivers. Thus, if we project a quarterback to score 300 points and a wide receiver to score 200, those value shift to $0.60(300)=180$ and $0.42(200)=84$, respectively. Note that those numbers aren't projected points, but rather weighted values that make comparisons of various players easier.

The primary problem with this method, in my view, is it values the consistent positions too greatly, widening the "scarcity" gap at these spots. For example, if we assume the 300-point quarterback and 200-point receiver are the top players at their respective positions and that our second-ranked players were projected to score 285 (QB) and 190 (WR), the above formula would change those projections to 171 and 79.

Whereas the second-ranked players were projected to score five percent less than their top-ranked counterparts in the original projections, the new consistency-infused projections have the second quarterback still at five percent behind the top signal-caller, but the second receiver 6.0 percent behind the top pass-catcher. In effect, multiplying position correlation strength by projected points increases the "scarcity" of the most consistent positions, improperly inflating their worth.

To compensate for this effect on scarcity, we can use a new formula that incorporates average points for each position. To obtain better projections, we can multiply the difference in projected points and average points by the aforementioned correlational strength of each position, then add that number to the average points. That is:

$C(P-A) + A$, where C is correlational strength, P is projected points, and A is average points for fantasy starters at the position

Let's assume we project a tight end to score 200 points and a wide receiver to score 220 points, with the average at the positions being 150 and 180, respectively. We could factor positional consistency into those projections by multiplying the difference between the projection and the average by 0.62 and 0.42, respectively. Our new projections would be:

Tight End: 0.62(200-150) + 150 = 181
Wide Receiver: 0.42(220-180) + 180 = 197

Since the positional scoring mean is incorporated into the formula, we can effectively control the effect of inflated scarcity that plagued the initial formula.

Using Projections to Create Tiers

Ranking your players into tiers is the easiest way to capitalize on VORP draft strategy, as it is a quick and effective way to recognize position scarcity. Adding tiers to your draft board is relatively straightforward, as you are looking for big jumps in projected points. Of course, things like season-to-season consistency and risk play a role, but the idea is to separate players based on the likelihood they perform well for you.

Let's take an example. For simplicity's sake, let's use the same quarterback projections I created earlier:

Drew Brees – 400 points Risk: 6/10
Aaron Rodgers – 395 points Risk: 1/10
Peyton Manning – 390 points Risk: 9/10
Tom Brady – 385 points Risk: 3/10
Cam Newton – 360 points Risk: 8/10
Matthew Stafford – 355 points Risk: 5/10
Tony Romo – 350 points Risk: 3/10

In this situation, it's pretty easy to see we should sort quarterbacks 1-4 into one tier, with quarterbacks 5-7 in another. But what if we were to swap the projected points for

Tom Brady and Cam Newton? Brady would rank fifth with 360 projected points, but he also carries very little risk.

In such a scenario, we could place Brady into the top tier, even potentially ranking him ahead of Newton based on his limited risk. There's no objective way to determine if you should place Brady at No. 4 or No. 5, but the point is things other than projected points should factor into your creation of tiers. Otherwise, we would mistakenly place Brady in the second tier and potentially miss out on a stud quarterback.

Tiers and Position Scarcity Can Lead to Counterintuitive Draft Decisions

It's the sixth round of your draft, and you've managed to land Ray Rice, Jimmy Graham, Hakeem Nicks, Fred Jackson, and Percy Harvin in the first five rounds. You're sitting pretty, but you really need a top signal-caller to cap off a ridiculous starting lineup. Your board looks like this:

QB Matt Ryan – 300 projected points (Tier 3)
QB Tony Romo – 295 projected points (Tier 3)
QB Philip Rivers – 290 projected points (Tier 3)
QB Eli Manning – 290 projected points (Tier 3)
RB DeAngelo Williams – 225 projected points (Tier 4)
WR Eric Decker – 180 projected points (Tier 6)
RB Peyton Hillis – 200 projected points (Tier 5)

With Matt Ryan sitting there and capable of rounding out your starting lineup, it seems impossible to pass on the Atlanta Falcon. It would be a huge mistake, however, as the correct choice is DeAngelo Williams. Despite already landing two running backs, including Ray Rice, Williams offers the most value.

Again, let's allow the math to show why. Assume you draft Ryan and his 300 projected points, content to gamble on Peyton Hillis in the seventh round. You know Williams will be off the board by the time your next pick rolls around, but you can't pass on your top-rated player. This Best Player Available draft strategy lands you 500 total projected points in Rounds 6-7.

If you utilize VORP and stick to your tiers, however, you can bypass maximum value to acquire Williams and his 225 projected points. If the draft stopped after six rounds, you might be in trouble. Luckily for you, it's a bit longer.

With eight quarterbacks drafted by eight different owners prior to your selection, you can be fairly certain one of your Tier 3 quarterbacks, Ryan, Romo, Rivers, or Manning, will be available in the seventh round. Despite obtaining only 225 projected points in the sixth round, your total for Rounds 6-7, using tier-based VORP draft strategy, would be 515 points even if you landed your last quarterback in Tier 3—15 points more than the Best Player Available draft strategy.

Thus, even though VORP can seem counterintuitive, in the long run, the strategy leads to better overall draft results than BPA. Here's another great example of VORP.

Understanding Opponent Beliefs with Game Theory
As I mentioned in my intro, game theory is a strategic decision-making process that applies to zero-sum games wherein the beliefs of others affect your decisions. Game theory has extreme implications to fantasy football draft strategies.

Thus far, I've assumed other owners in your fantasy leagues are completely rational. Obviously this isn't true, and in each fantasy draft there will be tons of "reaches" when players are selected far higher than consensus rankings. This doesn't mean the player chosen is a poor one, but rather that the choice is probably earlier than any other owner would have drafted him.

One of your jobs as a fantasy owner is to determine when other owners will draft specific players, both on a league-wide scale and an individual one. With regards to the latter, this can be completed by simply talking to other owners, figuring out which positions they value, and so on.

Unless you are in an expert league, you can be sure no other owners are using VORP draft strategy. This means they will be far more likely to fill in their starters prior to selecting any bench players, and you can use this knowledge to your advantage. When Uncle Bruce has selected a running back, wide receiver, and running back in the first three rounds, you can be sure he isn't taking another running back in the fourth.

Game Theory on a League-Wide Scale: Average Draft Position

You can use game theory in a broader way by projecting the draft positions of each player. One way to do this is a mock draft, although individual mock drafts are susceptible to fluctuations and randomness in a big way. Change one draft pick in an individual draft and you can drastically alter subsequent picks.

This is where Average Draft Position (ADP) comes in. ADP is simply a calculation of where each player is getting drafted in a given year. ADP is based on thousands of mock drafts, so the "noise" of an individual mock is leveled out. With ADP, you can get an idea of when Uncle Bruce plans to take the top rookie running back or the quarterback coming off ACL surgery. Since ADP is based on real mock drafts and the owners selecting in these drafts use the same draft guides as Uncle Bruce, it can give you a solid understanding of the intentions of your league owners.

Game theory, and ADP in particular, is the reason my dad was unjustified in selecting Matt Forte so high in 2010. It isn't that he was necessarily wrong, and it didn't matter, because the point is ADP allows you to acquire the players you want at the *correct* spots, allowing VORP to do its thing. For the most accurate ADP numbers, head here.

Why Drafting Near the End of a Round is Valuable

As a quick aside, I wanted to point out drafting near the end of rounds (but not as the last pick in a round) can allow for a few advantages. If you are in a 12-team league and you are allowed to pick your own draft spot, consider that spots 2, 3, 4, 9, 10, and 11 might have more intrinsic value than 1, 5, 6, 7, 8, and 12.

In snake drafts that use a reverse draft order for subsequent rounds, drafting near the end of a round allows you to accurately predict which players might get selected between your own picks. If you hold the 11th and 14th overall picks in a 12-team league, for example, you could easily bypass specific players in favor of others if you know the sole owner drafting between you doesn't need or want the player you intend to draft in the later round.

For instance, assume your pick is approaching in the fifth round and you are considering a running back and a quarterback. Only one person picks behind you before the round is over, and he already has two running backs, but no quarterback. In such a situation, it is easy to see why you should select the signal-caller, even if the running back is higher on your board.

Drafting in the middle of rounds doesn't afford you this advantage. Yes, you don't need to wait nearly two full rounds to make selections as is the case when drafting at the edge of rounds, but it isn't possible to predict the players to be selected between any of your picks anyway.

Regardless, it is obvious the first and last spots in any draft are inherently less valuable than other slots, as you have to wait extended periods of time between picks, yet you cannot benefit from game theory in regards to your draft spot.

The Bottom Line

- Projections are not only useful in creating accurate rankings, they are vital.

- We can implement both consistency and scarcity into our rankings with the following formula: 'C(P-A) + A,' where C is correlational strength, P is projected points, and A is average points for fantasy starters at the position

- Projections are the basis from which we can create power ratings and positional tiers, but they are not the only factor.

- Risk should also determine the formation of rankings.

- VORP involves taking the "scarcest" player at his respective position, even if it seems counterintuitive.

- Understanding your opponents' beliefs can lead to significant draft advantages.

- Average Draft Position is the easiest tool to understand public perception and subsequently enhance your implementation of game theory into VORP.

- Drafting near but not at the end of a round is intrinsically valuable because it increases your ability to predict players that will get drafted between your picks.

Chapter 5: More on Position Scarcity

Thus far, I have only glossed over position scarcity, instead opting to examine consistency in greater detail. One reason is identifying position scarcity is a natural product of creating projections. The act of formulating tiered rankings based on player stat projections is equivalent to dividing players based on scarcity. When you bypass a position of need because there are an abundance of players left in that position's tier, you are effectively employing scarcity within your draft strategy.

Nonetheless, I thought it would be worthwhile to examine overall scarcity levels by positions; that is, which positions are "top heavy" and should thus be selected early in draft? The two graphs below incorporate stats over a five-year period.

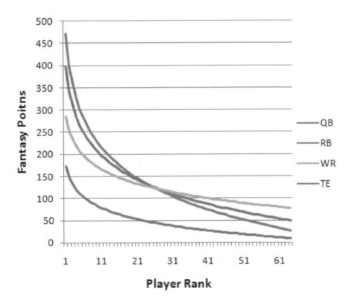

You can see the steepness of the curves is greatest for the quarterback and running back positions, followed by tight end and receiver. This seems to support my previous notion that quarterback and running back are the most important positions to land in the first round.

The scarcity of the quarterback and tight end spots intensifies when we factor consistency into the mix:

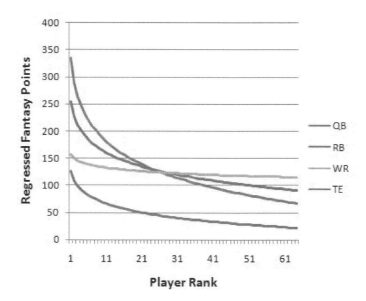

You can see the quarterback and tight end positions steepen, while the other two skill positions see their curves flatten out. Again, remember the correlation of year-to-year consistency is 0.62 for tight ends, 0.60 for quarterbacks, 0.48 for running backs, and 0.42 for wide receivers.

This scarcity and consistency-driven graph is a perfect example of why VORP is a better draft strategy than BPA. At no time do the wide receiver and tight end curves cross, yet the value added from a top-tier tight end is much greater than that from a top receiver. While no owner is going to be upset with Calvin Johnson on their team in 2012, Jimmy Graham will lead to more fantasy championships. The opportunity cost of bypassing him or the other top tight ends is much greater than forgoing the selection of a premiere wide out.

However, note the continued flatness of the wide receiver curve. You can see by around the 30th spot in player rank, wide receivers are the top scorers in fantasy football. There are gems to be had late in the draft at the receiver position, and this due to a combination low scarcity and a pass-happy NFL.

Aaron Rodgers and Rob Gronkowski: The Perfect 1-2 Punch?

In the graph above, you can literally see the strong combination of scarcity and consistency among the quarterback and tight end positions. The top running backs are important too, and the most consistent ones should be a consideration in the first round.

Season-to-season consistency is so important in the first couple of rounds because the upside of these picks, relative to their draft spot, is minimal. First-round selections are *supposed* to score a ton of points, which is why there are more "busts" in this round than any other; it is all about expectations. In essence, first-round picks are simply the outliers from the previous season; they likely overachieved, and are thus likely to regress in the current season.

With a ceiling that can't grow much higher than expectation, you can secure the most value in the initial rounds by minimizing the floor, or downside, or your picks. In other words, avoid volatility at all costs. **The later rounds, when ceilings are lower and starting lineups are filling out, is the time to gamble on high-upside players.**

In other words, the most successful owners tend to make the "boring" picks early. I've already discussed why quarterback and tight end are the two most predictable positions in fantasy football. For this reason, those who select in the middle of the first and second rounds should strongly consider grabbing the draft's top quarterback and tight end. As of this writing, the ADPs of Aaron Rodgers and Rob Gronkowski are 4.5 and 18.9, respectively.

Of course, the "correct" pick at each spot is really relative to your particular league (and I will have more later regarding how to alter your rankings based on league rules). Still, in most formats, Rodgers and Gronkowski (and a few similar players) possess value few other owners will realize, and it comes in the form of low volatility and high position scarcity.

The Bottom Line

- With scarcity in mind, it is generally suitable to draft quarterbacks and running backs in the first round.

- Grabbing a top-tier tight end in Rounds 2-4 is perhaps more valuable than selecting any other position in that range.

- You can find wide receiver talent late in the draft.

Chapter 6: Identifying Value: Regression, Randomness, and Running Backs

Back in 2008, I had running back Thomas Jones ranked well ahead of most owners. Jones was playing for the Jets and coming off a season in which he ran for 1,119 yards, but averaged just 3.6 yards-per-rush and scored only two total touchdowns. Those two scores represented just 0.59 percent of Jones' 338 touches in 2007.

ESPN had Jones ranked 21st among all running backs. I had him 10th. Why would I possibly rank a then 30-year old running back coming off a season in which he tallied 3.6 yards-per-carry and two total touchdowns in my top 10? Regression toward the mean.

Regression toward the mean is a phenomenon wherein "extreme" results tend to end up closer to the average on subsequent measurements. That is, a running back who garners 338 touches and scores only twice is far more likely to improve upon that performance than one who scored 25 touchdowns.

0-16 Detroit Lions: A Coach's Dream?

Regression to the mean is the reason the NFL coaches who take over the worst teams are in a far superior position to those who take over quality squads. If I were an NFL coach, there is no team I would prefer to take over more than the 2008 Detroit Lions. Coming off an 0-16 season, the Lions were almost assured improvement in 2009 simply because everything went wrong the previous season. Even though Detroit was a bad team, any coach who took over in 2009 was basically guaranteed to oversee improvement in following years.

This same sort of logic is the reason there are so many first-round "busts" in fantasy football. Players almost always get selected in the first-round because they had monster years in the prior season. In effect, most first-rounders are the "outliers" from the prior season's data, and their play is more likely to regress than improve in the current year. It isn't that these players are poor picks, but rather the combination of quality play, health, and other random factors that led to their prior success is unlikely to work out so fortunately again.

Players Aren't "Due"

Walk into any casino in America and you will see lines of hopeful grandmothers lining up behind slot machines that haven't paid recently. Since the machines pay a specific average of money over the course of their lives and these numbers always even out over the long run, surely an underperforming slot machine must be due to pay out soon, right?

This is one of the biggest misconceptions regarding statistics and regression, and it is the cause of millions of lost dollars each year. In a set of random data, previous occurrences have absolutely no effect on future events. If you flip a coin right now and it lands on heads, the chance it lands on heads again on your next flip is still 50 percent.

Similarly, if the overall payout rate of a slot machine is 40 percent, the most likely outcome of placing $1,000 into it is walking away with $400. You could walk away big or you (theoretically) could lose every penny, but the most probable single dollar amount you could "win" is $400. So when the previous 100 pulls of the lever are fruitless, the payout "improvement" that is likely to take place over the next 100 pulls isn't because the machine is "due," but rather it is simply working as normal. This is regression toward the mean.

But football isn't random.

Football isn't totally random, but it's more random than you think. Actually, some statisticians have estimated the "luck factor" to be as high as .924 in the NFL. That means on any given week, the "true" winning percentage of teams that win is really around .538. In a league in which only 16 games make up a season, the talent gap between teams is lessening, and turnovers play a huge role in wins, the amount of luck involved in the game is more so than any other professional sport.

Even disregarding the potential randomness of NFL outcomes, the identification of underperforming players can be of incredible value to fantasy owners. As it relates to Thomas Jones, it doesn't really matter how much randomness was involved in his two-touchdown season. Heading into the 2008 season as the workhorse back on a team with a strong offensive line and no real reason to think he was a fundamentally poor short-yardage runner, projecting Jones to score more than a handful of times was easy. I projected him at 10 touchdowns. He scored 15.

So when other owners are jumping all over the players who had "extreme" seasons the prior year, look for talented players who actually underperformed. As long as they get similar opportunities to make plays, their numbers will probably improve. For fantasy owners, this represents value.

Of course this doesn't mean you should select weaker players simply because they had poor years. In the first few rounds, you are almost certain to draft outliers who played better than normal the season before. Your job is to recognize which players' value is primarily the result of random factors, and thus likely to regress to the average, and which is based largely on talent, and thus likely to repeat itself.

How To Determine an "Average" Season

Of course, not every player has the same "average" season. If we were to simulate 1,000 NFL seasons, Ray Rice's per-season totals would obviously eclipse those of, say, Beanie Wells. So recognizing how players' stats will regress involves identifying (or at least intelligently estimating) their "average" season. In a typical season, how many more yards, touchdowns, and receptions will Rice score as compared to Wells? Until we establish mean seasons for each player, we have no base from which we can determine to where their numbers from the previous season will regress. That is, the totals for Rice and Wells aren't likely to regress to the mean for all backs, but rather they will regress to their specific averages.

Determining this value can be tricky. One of the easiest ways is to determine how many "lucky" plays a player benefited from in a specific year. We have already seen stats like interceptions are inherently fluky, and thus very likely to regress to the mean in subsequent seasons. Aaron Rodgers is a heck of a player, but he's very unlikely to match his 45:6 TD-to-INT ratio from 2011.

Other statistics, such as touchdowns and long-yardage plays, are not necessarily extremely random, but they can still have a major impact on fantasy scores. In Chris Johnson's 2009 season in which he broke the record for total yards from scrimmage, he totaled seven touchdowns of 50-plus yards. That number is the ninth best of all-time. . .for a career!

Despite possessing game-breaking speed, it would have been foolish to believe Johnson would repeat his 2009 campaign.

Our job as fantasy owners was to determine what an "average" Johnson season would look like, taking the extent of Johnson's 2009 "luck" into account.

Still, the task of predicting average seasons on an individual basis is a difficult one. There is no single method to do it, but understanding the inherent instability of interceptions, fumbles, long touchdowns, field goals, etc. is a start.

The Myth of Overworked Running Backs

One of the most frequent mistakes made by fantasy football owners is assuming all correlations are due to a causal effect. Lots of things in life are related, yet have no effect on one another. The old notion that great running teams win football games is an illusion based on a misunderstanding of the correlation/causation distinction, for example. Yes, winning teams average more rushing yards than losing teams, but that's because teams that are *already winning* run the ball late in games. In reality, they usually gain the lead by passing the football effectively.

A prevalent fantasy football "truism" is the idea that overworked running backs struggle in subsequent seasons. There are numerous studies out there detailing how running backs struggle when coming off a season with 350 touches, or 370 touches, or however many touches is necessary for the study to make sense. The exact number is usually chosen ex post facto and is to be regarded as a "magical threshold" that spells doom in the following season if crossed.

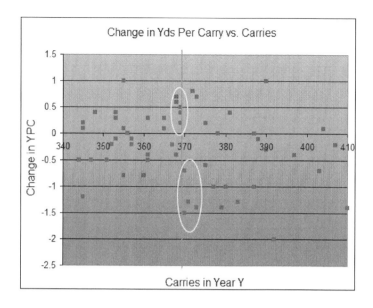

The graph above shows you just how silly some of this analysis can get. In a study on the effect of 370-plus carries on running backs, the number seems to be chosen after the fact because it makes the numbers more extreme. You can see the abundance of running backs that actually improved their yards-per-carry, yet came just a few carries short of 370. Are we really to believe a running back who carried the ball 365 times in a season is to be trusted in the subsequent season, but those with 370 are doomed?

In reality, though, **running backs who garner a large number of touches in a season are generally more likely to see a drop in production and health in the following year, but this information is both insignificant and irrelevant.**

Think about what it takes to acquire nearly 400 touches in a season. For one, a running back needs to be healthy. Really healthy. Secondly, chances are he is running efficiently. Running backs who average 3.5 yards-per-carry over the first half of the season don't generally continue to see the 24 carries a game needed to break the 370 threshold. Thus, our sample size of high-carry backs is skewed by those performing well.

This is where regression toward the mean comes in. By filtering out injured and underperforming backs, selecting those with a high number of carries means we are selecting the outliers in more areas than one. We aren't isolating the numbers based on carries, but rather based on health and efficiency as well. So when we make conclusions concerning health and efficiency, all we're really saying is players who have unusual health and a higher-than-normal YPC are likely to have worse health and a lower YPC the following year. Uh, yeah. . .no crap.

So yeah, **running backs with a lot of carries in year Y usually see a drop in production in year+1, but it's a product of regression, not a heavy workload.** The graph below supports this idea.

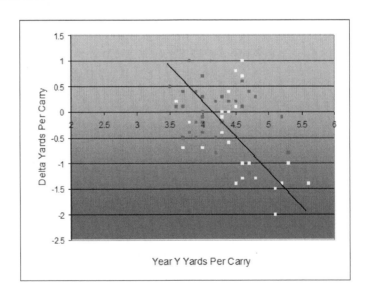

You can see the efficiency of *all* running backs tends to regress to the mean, not just those coming off seasons with heavy workloads. If a back runs for 6.0 YPC in a year, he will probably see a decline in efficiency whether he had 50 carries or 400.

Thus, **while the production of a running back coming off a season with a heavy workload is likely to decrease, it is not a legitimate reason to avoid that player in fantasy drafts.** The (probable) decrease in production is due to the previous season being a statistical outlier (a result that is unusually far from the mean).

The best way to look at the situation is this: what is the running back's chance of generating production that is comparable to the previous year? It is actually *the same* as it was prior to the start of the previous season, i.e. the workload has no noticeable effect on his ability to produce.

For example, if a running back has a 20 percent chance of garnering 2,000 total yards in a season, that percentage remains stable (assuming his skills level does the same) from year to year. Thus, the chance of this player following a 2,000 yard season with another is unlikely, but not due to a heavy workload (a necessity for such productive output), but rather the fact that he only had a 20 percent chance to do so from the start. We wrongly (and ironically) attribute the decrease in production to the player's prior success when, in reality, no such causal relationship exists.

How to Predict Running Backs' Yards-Per-Carry

As I wrote earlier, fantasy owners need to determine which aspects of players' games are repeatable, and which are a matter of luck. Understanding the position consistency I detailed in previous sections is a start, and it gives us a foundation from which we can make projections of specific statistics.

Regression toward the mean is a factor in all projections. Rather than simply arbitrarily guessing projections, there are formulas we can use to make more educated predictions (albeit still "guesses"). To exemplify the magnitude of regression in projections, let's examine how to go about predicting a running back's yards-per-carry.

It turns out yards-per-carry has a <u>correlation strength of about 0.43</u> from season to season. That number is similar to the 0.50 correlational strength we saw with year-to-year rushing yards-per-game. It also means a large aspect of predicting running backs' YPC is simply accounting for the "luck" they experienced the season before.

After all is said and done, we can accurately predict YPC with the following formula:

$$YPC\_n+1 = LgAvgYPC -0.04+0.43*(YrNDiff)$$

In layman's terms, the most accurate YPC projection we can make is taking 3/7 of the previous year's YPC and adding it to 4/7 of the league average (about 4.2), then subtracting 0.04. For a running back who averaged 6.0 yards-per-carry, the projection would be 6.0 (3/7) + 4.2 (4/7) – 0.04 = 4.93 YPC.

Notice the formula will decrease the projected YPC of any back who registered above 4.2, but increase the YPC of anyone below that figure. A back who mustered only 3.8 YPC in year Y is most likely to total 3.8 (3/7) + 4.2 (4/7) – 0.04 = 3.99 YPC in year Y+1.

There will be more information on projecting specific stats for each position in following analysis. A lot of this will be based on regression toward the mean, but there are certainly a lot of other factors at play. It is important to remember these formulas aren't a definitive source for final projections, but rather a solid base from which to work.

The Bottom Line

- Regression to the mean states "extreme" events tend to regress toward the average, and fantasy owners can use it to acquire value. Just as traders buy low and sell high, fantasy owners can pinpoint which players are due for boosts or declines in production based on how much of their previous production was caused by random factors.

- Your job as an owner isn't to select players who had poor seasons, but rather those who are being undervalued due to production that was below their "average season." In effect, you are buying low on players whose value will "regress" upward.

- Regression toward the mean shows us running backs coming off seasons with heavy workloads are likely to see a decline in production, but not because of the workload itself. Instead, these backs are necessarily the outliers from the previous season, and statistically likely to regress. In practical terms, it means there's no reason for owners to purposely avoid running backs who had a lot of touches the prior season.

- One of the easiest and most accurate ways to predict a running back's yards-per-carry is to multiply his YPC from the previous year by 3/7, then add that number by 4/7 of the league average YPC (which works out to 2.4), then subtract 0.04. Other factors are of course relevant, but this is a great foundation from which to work.

Chapter 7: Getting Bullish: What the Stock Market Can Teach Us About Fantasy Football

Thus far, I've discussed the concept of value quite a bit. But what is value, as it relates to fantasy football? How can a running back projected for 300 points be a poor value pick in the first round, yet one projected to score 175 points be tremendous value in the 15th round?

Opportunity Cost

As I write this section, the Eagles are attempting to trade cornerback Asante Samuel, without much success. There are rumors no team will yield more than a late-round selection for the cornerback. Samuel is past his prime, but he's certainly still a starting-caliber defensive back. He yielded just a 52.4 passer rating in 2011 (fifth-best in the NFL), and Pro Football Focus graded Samuel as the league's 12th best player at the position.

If the NFL invoked an economic structure similar to that of Major League Baseball, Samuel would have plenty of potential suitors. In a league without a salary cap, the cost of players extends only so far as the owner's checkbook. Many of baseball's billionaire owners don't mind overspending in order to secure elite players. If money is no object, the value of baseball players relates only to their ability to play well.

In the NFL, however, teams are limited by a strict enforcement of a salary cap. The cost of signing players is greater due to the actual contract, its hindrance on a team's salary cap management, and the inability of an organization to sign other players. All of these aspects make up the opportunity cost of having a player on your team.

As it relates to Samuel, the Eagles owe him $21.5 million over the next two years. Even though Samuel is a good cornerback, his performance and age probably don't warrant that kind of money. Assuming owner Jeffrey Lurie doesn't mind shelling out $21.5 million to Samuel from a financial standpoint, the figure is still a blow to Philly's salary cap, and it blocks their ability to sign other players. Despite being a quality player, Samuel isn't of particularly great value to the Eagles.

Finding Value in Fantasy Drafts

For fantasy owners, the round in which a player is selected represents his "contract." Thus, a single player can possess both great and horrible value depending where he gets drafted, with the opportunity cost being the loss of the pick. Later rounds represent a lower opportunity cost.

The job of fantasy owners is to acquire the most possible value with each selection by decreasing the opportunity cost as much as possible.

Value Isn't Inherent

We know a player's value in the NFL and fantasy football isn't based solely on his projected performance, but also the opportunity cost of acquiring him. A vital aspect of this idea is that different players can hold various amounts of value for different teams.

Let's go back to Samuel. His contract is the primary reason the Eagles are willing to let him walk, but another important factor is the Eagles roster. With Nnamdi Asomugha and Dominique Rodgers-Cromartie also at cornerback, Samuel's potential value to the team is minimal at his $21.5 million price tag. If a team ends up trading for Samuel, it will likely be one without a strong group of cornerbacks. For them, $21.5 million may not represent an overpayment (meaning Samuel's opportunity cost is reduced, and he thus holds more value).

Just as a player's fantasy value alters based on his draft spot, it also can fluctuate depending on which owner selects him. Let's head to the third round of your upcoming fantasy draft. You've managed to land Ray Rice and Adrian Peterson in the first two rounds, and Matt Forte has somehow fallen to your pick in the third.

For most owners, Forte would represent incredible value. For you, not so much. The opportunity cost of selecting Forte is monumental, as you would be forced to again bypass the selection of other positions. Forte's projected points might be substantial, but the points he'll be projected to score for your squad would be minimal.

While players clearly don't have a totally objective value, they do possess a semi-objective value as it relates to your team (based on your rankings). To forgo the selection of a "need" position, the player you draft must possess great semi-objective value. Thus, **"value" picks aren't as straightforward as they seem; the value of a selection isn't based only on what you acquire, but also what you _don't_.**

Why You Rarely Draft the Best Player Available

That last sentence is an important one, as it highlights the primary vindication of VORP draft strategy over Best Player Available. A few sections ago, I wrote:

> Any worthwhile draft strategy must possess an overarching vision; draft strategies like "Best Player Available" are too shortsighted, unnecessarily limiting

the projected points you can acquire down the road in favor of more now.

Projecting future picks is not only an important component of understanding opportunity cost, but also an intrinsic one. The cost of drafting any particular player, then, comes not only with the loss of a pick, but also in the inability to select other players, both at the current selection and future ones.

In some ways, opportunity cost is simply a different way to look at VORP. Fantasy owners must perform the delicate task of minimizing opportunity cost by selecting players with value, i.e. those who are scarce, predictable, and needed.

Minimizing "Lost" Points
You may have noticed a different type of mindset developing here. Whereas most fantasy owners are concerned about acquiring the most possible projected points with each pick, your focus should be "losing" the least. If the perfect fantasy team represents the acquisition of the most possible total projected points, your job is to minimize the loss of projected points at each selection, and this minimization requires forward-thinking. The more shortsighted BPA strategy does not. This concept is known as **minimax.**

Fantasy Football as a Stock Market
A fantasy football draft is really no different than the stock market. Both stock traders and fantasy owners seek to leverage knowledge into value acquisition, and that value is the result of cost minimization. And just as game theory is a useful tool in the fantasy owner's arsenal, a fundamental understanding of public perception is vital to traders.

Stocks are not inherently good or bad. Rather, those designations come in relation to the price of the stock. The value of Microsoft stock, for example, has no meaning without knowledge of the share price. Microsoft is currently selling at around $32 per share. Buying at $20 is probably a smart move; buying at $50 likely is not so wise.

Likewise, **players are not valuable to fantasy owners outside of a proper understanding of their opportunity cost.** Adrian Peterson, coming off reconstructive knee surgery, isn't great value in the first round this year. In the third round, however, he could be a steal.

Buy Low, Sell High

The goal of investors is to sell stocks at their peak and buy them at their lowest point. When a stock is at its highest price, that number is likely not representative of the stock's true worth. In most cases, stocks tend to fall after they reach an all-time high due to regression toward the mean.

Similarly, **fantasy owners are in the business of "buying" players whose perceived value is lower than their actual value, and "selling" players whose perceived value *exceeds* their actual value.** I talked about this a bit before when describing how it's useful to recognize which of a player's stats are due to random events, and thus likely to regress. This "buy low, sell high" mentality is fundamental to stock trading and fantasy drafting.

Understanding Public Perception

At the heart of the value determination process for both traders and fantasy owners is a keen knowledge of public perception. **Traders seek to predict which stocks will become popular among the public prior to that stock's share price rising.**

Similarly, fantasy owners must recognize which players have too low of a price tag (or Average Draft Position). Both share price and ADP are set by the public.

To exemplify the importance of understanding public perception and how to utilize it in fantasy football, consider the interaction between bookmakers and sports bettors. Contrary to what many people believe, bookmakers don't generally set lines based on actual games. Rather, game lines are determined by how the bookmakers anticipate bets rolling in. If the public thinks the Cowboys are a seven-point favorite but the book knows they should really be a three-point underdog, they'll still set the line closer to the Cowboys being a seven-point favorite because, over the long run, that will create a better return for them.

Professional sports bettors know they don't need to necessarily beat the book, but rather they need to beat the public. The most efficient way to do this is recognize which game factors are vital to the outcome but not typically known by the public, and thus not implemented into the line.

Similarly, traders and fantasy owners must understand how the public perceives stocks and football players to enhance value. For the latter group, the worth comes in not knowing which players to draft, but more importantly, *when* to draft them. Remember, neither stocks nor players have inherent value; value is a reflection of both actual worth and opportunity cost, the latter trait being influenced heavily by public perception.

How to Exploit Hidden Stats

Back in my analysis of consistency, I noted how important quarterback rushing yards can be to fantasy owners. In addition to being predictable, I wrote:

"Hidden" stats like quarterback rushing yards are an opportunity for wise owners to gain an advantage. Many write off quarterback rushing yards as inconsequential, but they can be leveraged into an advantage in the same way sports bettors utilize factors that aren't already in the betting line to correctly beat the spread.

Think of it this way. . .although an injured quarterback certainly has a huge effect on the outcome of a game, it does little to affect a bettor's ability to beat the spread, since the injury is already factored into the line. An injured center also affects a game in a substantial way, but this injury is far more valuable to a bettor because it is unlikely to influence the spread.

In a similar way, stats like passing yards are already factored into consensus rankings. By using "hidden" stats like quarterback rushing yards, you can identify true value in a superior manner to your opponents. And you only need to beat your Uncle Bruce, not Vegas.

Quarterback rushing yards are a component of total fantasy points, but many other stats are not. Handoffs inside the five-yard line and red zone targets, for example, aren't necessarily reflected in a player's fantasy points. Still, these "hidden" stats are a way to determine if a player's actual value is equivalent to his perceived value, potentially providing an owner with an opportunity to leverage the numbers into a competitive advantage. While stats like touchdowns are obviously more valuable in terms of fantasy points scored, they're already factored into Uncle Bruce's rankings, and thus not a means of exploitation.

Like the stock market, fantasy football drafts are an opportunity for wise "traders" to recognize value, exploiting weaknesses in an inefficient market by "buying low" on stocks (or players) the public (or players in your league) deems less valuable than what you know to be the case. In the next section, I will discuss how to use consistency, "hidden" stats, and other factors to create projections and overall draft philosophies for each position.

The Bottom Line
- Value is a measure of the ratio of a player's projected points versus the opportunity cost to draft him. Opportunity cost includes everything you must surrender to draft a player, including the pick and the players you bypass. What you must forgo with a pick is just as important as what you acquire.

- Fantasy draft strategies must possess an overarching vision to maximize total projected points. The task of predicting future picks via an implementation of opportunity cost is not only a vital part of VORP, but also an essential one. BPA doesn't advocate this forward thinking.

- Fantasy football drafts are much like the stock market in a number of key areas. Both owners traders look "buy low."

- Players aren't inherently valuable, but only insofar as their true worth exceeds their perceived worth and the opportunity cost of drafting them. Thus, recognizing public opinion is necessary for owners to generate maximum value. This relates back to our discussion of game theory.

- Uncovering stats that are predictive of a player's future production, yet not implemented into consensus rankings, can often be more valuable to fantasy owners than assessing the "big" stats like yards and touchdowns.

Chapter 8: The Ultimate Draft Plan: From Projections to Selections

Thus far, the majority of the book has dealt with the philosophy of drafting, including the best methodologies for projecting points, formulating rankings, and selecting players. In short, I showed you the 'why,' but now I want to display the 'how.' But just *how* are we to go about utilizing what we've learned within the structure of an all-encompassing draft strategy? Below, I will provide specific details on how to create an overarching draft plan, from projections to selections.

Projection Philosophy: Why Projections Matter, But Don't Really Matter

What!? More philosophy!? Just a little. . .

To create projections for each position, we need only use a variation of the formula I gave you to predict running backs' yards-per-carry. That was "YPC_n+1 = LgAvgYPC - 0.04+0.43*(YrNDiff)," wherein 0.43 represents the strength of the year-to-year consistency of running backs' yards-per-rush.

To project quarterbacks' passing yards, we simply take their yardage total from the previous season and multiply it by the strength of the correlation between year-to-year passing yard totals, then add that total to [1-(strength of correlation)](average total passing yards).

If you remember from a few chapters ago, the strength of correlation for passing yards is 0.50. That's basically another way of saying that, on average, half a quarterback's yards are due to skill, and half are due to luck. Thus, if Quarterback A threw for 4,000 yards in 2011, we can assume 2,000 were due to skill.

That total of 2,000 then gets added to the "league average" for quarterback passing totals. Unlike running back yards-per-carry, however, we cannot use the true league average since not every quarterback participates in every game. Further, we only care about the average *fantasy* quarterback.

Determining the "average" player at a position is an easy way to factor starting requirements for your league into your rankings. The more starters that are required at a specific position, the lower the average fantasy starter will score at that spot. In a hypothetical league that starts four quarterbacks, the average score for a fantasy starter would be quite low. By having a low average, it increases the value of the position because good quarterbacks will be well ahead of the average in terms of projected passing yards, thus making them scarcer. As opposed to a position where most players are near the league average, a position with outliers, as we learned in prior chapters, is one we want to target.

For our purposes, the statistics we will examine to determine an "average" player at each position will coincide with the number of total fantasy starters in the league. So, if you are in a 12-team league and start one quarterback, your "average" quarterback, in terms of passing yards, will be whoever ranked 12th in yards the previous season. In 2011, that player was Joe Flacco with 3,610 yards.

Now that we have established a baseline, we can finish our equation. Since half of a quarterback's yards are due to skill and half are due to luck, we simply need to take 50% of their previous season's total (which we determined is 2,000 for our hypothetical quarterback) and add it to 50% of the average (which turns out to be 1,805 yards). Thus, a quarterback who threw for 4,000 yards in 2011 would be projected yards it throw for 3,805 yards in 2012.

At this point, you might be asking a very important question. If a player's projected totals are based on league averages, wouldn't they change if we used a different average? The answer is yes, but it is actually irrelevant.

Remember, it is not the point projections that matter in fantasy football, but rather the relationship between each player's points and other players at his position. It doesn't matter if you project a player to score 10,000 points if there are other options available at 9,999 points. By altering the projections based on flexible league averages, you can automatically create values that take your league starting requirements into account, so you won't need to worry about them later. Don't forget that the end goal of creating projections isn't to perfectly predict cumulative stats, but rather to determine the most valuable players to select in your draft. Paradoxically, the stats don't matter and are everything simultaneously.

Going back to our example, let's assume you are in a league that starts two quarterbacks. Then, our "league average" quarterback won't be 12th-ranked Joe Flacco, but rather 24th-ranked Matt Schaub (who threw for 2,479 yards). Thus, Quarterback A, who threw for 4,000 yards in 2011, would be projected to throw for 2,000 + 1,239.5 yards in 2012, or about 3,240 yards.

If our projection of Quarterback A is lower (3,805 yards versus 3,240 yards), how could he possibly hold more value to us? Again, the points themselves don't matter. Although Quarterback A's passing yards projection drops in a league with two starting quarterbacks, the gap between his total and the average total increases. In our one-quarterback league, the gap is just 195 yards. In our two-quarterback league, it jumps substantially to 761 yards. In terms of fantasy football draft philosophy, the scarcity of Quarterback A soars in a two-quarterback league; that notion fits well with common sense, as we all know the extreme importance of quarterbacks in leagues that require two starters.

How to Project Quarterbacks

I just explained why the formula for projecting quarterback passing yards is 50% of the previous year's total plus 50% of the league average, as determined by your league's starting requirements. To produce the formulas for the other quarterback statistics, we need the strength of correlation numbers and league averages (for 12-team leagues in 2012):

Quarterback Correlations

Passing Yards: 0.50
Passing Touchdowns: 0.37
Interceptions: 0.08
Rushing Yards: 0.78
Rushing Touchdowns: 0.50

Quarterback League Averages

Passing Yards: 3,610 (one starter), 2,479 (two starters)
Passing Touchdowns: 21 (one starter), 13 (two starters)
Interceptions: 9 (one starter), 14 (two starters)
Rushing Yards: 128 (one starter), 79 (two starters)
Rushing Touchdowns: 2 (one starters), 1 (two starters)

Quarterback Projection Example

So let's project a player from last season. We'll take Matt Ryan, who threw for 4,177 yards, 29 touchdowns and 12 interceptions, and ran for 84 yards and two scores. Let's pretend he's in a one-quarterback league.

To project Matty Ice's passing yards, we add 50% of 4,177 (2,088.5) and 50% of the league average in a one-quarterback league (1,805) for a total of about 3,894 yards.

To predict his passing touchdowns, add 37% of 29 (10.7) to 63% of 21 (13.2) for a total of 24 touchdowns.

Interceptions are calculated by adding 8% of 12 (1.0) to 92% of nine (8.3) for a total of 9.3. We use the same methodology for rushing yards and touchdowns to get 94 yards and two touchdowns.

Thus, our initial 2012 projection for Matt Ryan is 4,177 passing yards, 24 touchdowns, 9.3 interceptions, 94 rushing yards and two rushing touchdowns.

Is that really it?

Obviously there is more that goes into projecting players than simply plugging their statistics from the previous season into a formula. However, too many owners create projections that mirror the previous season, not properly factoring regression toward the mean into the equation. **The projections you create with the formulas I have given you naturally account for regression, but they are to be used only as a solid baseline from which to work.**

In reality, a lot more goes into projecting stats. As I said earlier, your job is to recognize how closely a player's ability and situation with his team (i.e. offensive coordinator, teammate strength, injuries, etc.) resemble the league average fantasy player. Aaron Rodgers probably won't throw just six interceptions again in 2012, but he's probably more likely to be around that number than the two-quarterback fantasy league average of 14. Consider yourself a fantasy sculptor. Assessing each player's true talent and ability to succeed is the tool by which you can mold the initial fantasy projections.

Projecting The Other Positions

The same method is used to generate initial projections for the other primary fantasy positions. Listed below are the strength of correlations and league averages (based on 12 teams) for each position.

Running Back Correlations

Rushing Yards: 0.50
Rushing Touchdowns: 0.50
Receptions: 0.54
Receiving Yards: 0.51
Receiving Touchdowns: 0.29

Running Back Averages

Rushing Yards: 781 (two starters), 587 yards (three starters)
Rushing Touchdowns: 6 (two starters), 4 (three starters)
Receptions: 29 (two starters), 23 (three starters)
Receiving Yards: 267 (one starter), 187 (two starters)
Receiving Touchdowns: 1 (two and three starters)

Wide Receiver Correlations

Receiving Yards:0.58
Receiving Touchdowns:0.38
Receptions: 0.64

Wide Receiver Averages

Receiving Yards: 947 yards (two starters), 757 yards (three starters)
Receiving Touchdowns: 7 (two starters), 5 touchdowns (three starters)
Receptions: 65 (two starters), 54 (three starters)

Tight End Correlations

Receiving Yards:0.74
Receiving Touchdowns:0.44
Receptions: 0.65

Tight End Averages:

Receiving Yards: 767 (one starter)
Receiving Touchdowns: 5 (one starter)
Receptions: 59 (one starter)

But what about defenses and kickers?

Not everything in fantasy football needs to be so complex. I've shown defenses and kickers have almost zero predictability, so there's really no reason to take them earlier than the final two rounds. Pick one of each that you like. That's really it.

Using the consistency formulas I provided you as a foundation for projections, we're ready to mold our initial projections into final projections. To exemplify how to do this, I will analyze two players—Matt Ryan and Steve Smith.

Breaking Down Matt Ryan

As stated above, the initial projections have Ryan at 4,177 passing yards, 24 touchdowns, 9.3 interceptions, 94 rushing yards and two rushing touchdowns. Again, the exact numbers don't matter. Rather, we want to predict whether Ryan's stats from 2011 will increase or decrease in 2012, and to what extent, based on how much closely he performed to "average" Matt Ryan last season and how much he is expected to progress this season.

For players who have been in the league a few years, it is smart to take a gander at statistics from previous seasons. This can give us a clue as to how much Ryan's 2011 deviated from "the norm," as well as whether he is on the rise or decline.

Ryan posted career-high marks in passing yards, passing touchdowns, and rushing touchdowns in 2011. A lot of that had to do with the addition of Julio Jones. Jones is an elite receiver who will progress greatly in 2012, and his presence is a continuation of the transition of Atlanta's offense from a run-dominant attack to pass-heavy one. The past two seasons, Ryan threw well over 100 more passes than in his first two in the league. That trend will continue in 2012.

Ryan's yards-per-pass of 7.4 is about where we'd expect him to be in 2012, so we shouldn't see much regression in terms of passing yards. Jones will post better numbers, but his targets will likely come at the expense of Roddy White, i.e. Ryan's stats won't be affected too much.

Matty Ice has put up 16, 22, 28, and 29 touchdowns, respectively, in his first four seasons. He might throw another touchdown or two, but he almost certainly won't run for two scores again. Based on his career path thus far, his interceptions figure to again be in the 10-12 range. Ultimately, it looks like we can expect Ryan's numbers to remain pretty steady in 2012.

The purpose of this thought process was to determine if we should alter the baseline projections for Ryan (which happen to be different than my *actual* predictions for him). The answer is no. Even though I think Ryan will post better numbers than 4,177 passing yards and 24 touchdowns (our initial projections), it is the relation of these statistics to others at his position that matters.

By regressing Ryan's statistics based on league averages (as I did in the initial projections), it actually creates a larger point differential between Ryan and lesser quarterbacks, ultimately increasing Ryan's value. In two-quarterback leagues in which acquiring quarterbacks is vital, the importance of selecting signal-callers is reflected in the projections with this method. When simply projecting players in a traditional way, league starter requirements aren't represented in the rankings, potentially leading to a sub-optimal draft pick.

Breaking Down Steve Smith

Last year, Smith posted 79 receptions for 1,394 yards and seven touchdowns. Smith's yardage total was nearly the same as the previous two seasons combined, and a huge reason for that success was due to rookie quarterback Cam Newton.

When we plug Smith's stats into our equations, we get the following results (in a 12-team league that starts two receivers):

Receptions: 79(0.64) + 65(0.36) = 72.2
Yards: 1,394(0.58) + 947(0.42) = 1,206.3
Touchdowns: 7(0.38) + 7(0.62) = 7.0

Using Smith's 2011 numbers, the receiver strength of correlations, and the league averages, we see Smith's initial projection is 72 catches for 1,206 yards and seven touchdowns.

However, there is a lot of evidence out there that Smith is due to regress in 2012. He's 33 years old and playing with a quarterback who will likely go through some sort of sophomore slump (not because I believe in those things, but rather because Newton was rather "lucky" in 2011, at least as a passer). Even if Smith posts the same number of receptions and touchdowns, he'll be unlikely to match his 2011 mark of 17.3 yards-per-catch.

Further, Smith was targeted 129 times in 2011. That number might remain steady in 2012, but Smith will be unlikely to match his 61.2% catch rate from last season. Of the top 20 receivers in targets last season, only Wes Welker, Victor Cruz, and Percy Harvin posted a higher rate. With 129 targets and a more realistic catch rate of 56.0%, Smith's reception total would dip from 79 to 72.

Thus, we need to refine Smith's numbers a bit. Don't worry that the initial projections are already lower than Smith's 2011 stats—that relationship is irrelevant. Don't forget, the initial projections aren't meant to be accurate for 2012, but rather they are to be used as a comparison to other players at the same position.

Taking Smith's likelihood to regress into account, I envision a 2012 season of a few less receptions, a bunch less yards, and probably about the same number of touchdowns. Instead of

72/1,206/7, my projection for Smith in 2012 will look more like 65/1,050/7. Again, that's not to say I think Smith will wind up with those totals, but rather that will be the final projection I will use prior to creating wide receiver rankings.

Turning Stat Projections Into a Point Rating System

I've written again and again that fantasy owners aren't in the business of creating accurate stat projections, but rather accurate rankings. . .because it is a really important point. Our rankings are guided by some sort of total point projections, though, so why not just start with the latter (as opposed to stat projections) to create the former?

The reason is we need a method that will allow us to account for league scoring differences. **Turning stat projections into points is very simple. If your league awards four points for a passing touchdown, multiply projected passing touchdowns by four.** If it gives one point per 10 receiving yards, just divide projected receiving yards by 10. Straight brain surgery.

Turning Points Into Rankings

You can **think of the "projected points" you assign each player as more of a power ranking system.** Since the projected stats aren't meant to be accurate, neither are the projected points. **The relationship between points for players at each position, however, is far more relevant and allows for greater predictive power than other point projections.** Thus, think of the points you assign each player as more of a rating than a projection.

Once you develop power ratings for each player, you can begin the process of ranking them into tiers using the method I described near the start of the book. If you recall, you'll want to provide each player with a "risk rating" from one to 10. **After listing all players in each position based on their power rating** and then subsequently breaking each position into tiers, re-rank the players within each tier inversely according to their risk. Guess what? You just formulated a draft board.

The Ultimate Draft Board: The Big Picture

By creating initial projections that can change based on the number of teams in your league and the number of starters at each position, you'll eliminate the need to subjectively implement these factors later, instead opting for a system that is inherently cognizant of scarcity. Once you alter your initial projections to account for regression toward the mean, you'll have the base for rankings that are more representative of a player's true value than the statistics he put up the previous season.

Plugging in your league's scoring requirements and providing each player with a power rating will allow you to create an initial board, and you can tinker with that board by creating tiers and then rearranging those tiers based on the risk associated with each player.

All in all, this complex-but-accurate draft strategy takes care of the "Big Four" pillars of fantasy draft strategy: starting/scoring requirements, standard deviation/position scarcity, game theory, and consistency.

The Bottom Line

- You can create solid initial projections with a player's stats from last year, the year-to-year consistency of each stat for each position, and the "average" of each stat for your particular fantasy league.

- For fantasy owners, using the previous season's total of the player who would be the *last* fantasy starter in your league provides adequate rankings, i.e. if your 12-team league starts three wide receivers, use the 2011 receptions total of the 36th -ranked wide receiver (in terms of receptions only) as your "average" player.

- Altering the "average" player based on your league transforms stat projections, but your job as a fantasy owner isn't to create accurate projections. Rather, it is to assemble a great team via the draft. This method produces an accurate relationship between players at each position because it automatically factors position scarcity and your league's starting requirements into the mix.

- Once you make initial stat projections, you can tinker with them based on how representative last year's stats were to each player. For those due for a regression toward the mean (whether it is due to over-performance, a coaching change, or something else), either increase or decrease their totals. A running back who garnered an abundance of carries inside the opponent's five-yard line but scored only once in 2011 would be extremely likely to total more touchdowns in 2012, for example.

- Use your final stat projections to create a power rating system by plugging in your league's scoring. If you project a quarterback to throw for 4,000 yards and your league gives one point per 25 passing yards, you'll obviously award him with 160 points.

- Worry about the difference in points between players at each individual position, but not about the difference in points among players at different positions. Position scarcity (or the gap between the top-ranked player at a position and the next best you could secure later in the draft) is what should be on your mind while drafting.

- You can transform your power ratings into a draft board by breaking down each position into tiers (using scarcity). Then, assign each player a "risk rating" from one to 10, and rank each tier inversely based on risk.

Chapter 9: Don't Mock Me. Oh, now wait. . .

Yeah, that title is for real. Whatever. Mock drafts are essential to your fantasy draft prep. You can use mock drafts and ADP to help you implement game theory, i.e. knowing who to pick and when to pick them. Further, you can practice drafting from different slots to help you formulate your draft day plan.

As the final chapter in "Fantasy Football for Smart People," I wanted to take you through a few mock drafts I recently completed at Fantasy Football Calculator. The first draft below is in a 10-team league, and the final two are in 12-team leagues. All leagues are PPR (point per reception), and they all start 1 QB, 2 RB, 2 WR, 1 TE, 1 Flex, 1 K, and 1 D. I drafted from the first, fourth, and seventh draft spots, respectively, to give you an idea of what kind of talent you can get in various draft positions.

Mock Draft #1

1	2	3	4	5	6	7	8	9	10
LeSean McCoy RB (PHI) 7	Arian Foster RB (HOU) 8	Ray Rice RB (BAL) 3	Calvin Johnson WR (DET) 3	Maurice Jones-Drew RB (JAC) 6	Aaron Rodgers QB (GB) 10	Ryan Mathews RB (SD) 7	Chris Johnson RB (TEN) 11	Darren McFadden RB (OAK) 5	DeMarco Murray RB (DAL) 6
Andre Johnson WR (HOU) 8	Tom Brady QB (NE) 9	Roddy White WR (ATL) 7	Larry Fitzgerald WR (ARI) 10	Jamaal Charles RB (KC) 7	Trent Richardson RB (CLE) 10	Marshawn Lynch RB (SEA) 11	Jimmy Graham TE (NO) 6	Rob Gronkowski TE (NE) 9	Adrian Peterson RB (MIN) 11
Drew Brees QB (NO) 5	Matt Forte RB (CHI) 6	Steven Jackson RB (STL) 9	Darren Sproles RB (NO) 6	Michael Turner RB (ATL) 7	Fred Jackson RB (BUF) 8	Brandon Marshall WR (CHI) 6	Frank Gore RB (SF) 9	Hakeem Nicks WR (NYG) 11	Cam Newton QB (CAR) 6
Reggie Bush RB (MIA) 7	Aaron Hernandez TE (NE) 9	Victor Cruz WR (NYG) 11	Roy Helu RB (WAS) 10	Jordy Nelson WR (GB) 10	Beanie Wells RB (ARI) 10	Ahmad Bradshaw RB (NYG) 11	Wes Welker WR (NE) 9	Matthew Stafford QB (DET) 5	Greg Jennings WR (GB) 10
Mike Wallace WR (PIT) 4	A.J. Green WR (CIN) 6	Shonn Greene RB (NYJ) 9	Michael Vick QB (PHI) 7	Jermichael Finley TE (GB) 10	Dez Bryant WR (DAL) 5	Antonio Gates TE (SD) 7	Doug Martin RB (TB) 5	Julio Jones WR (ATL) 7	BenJarvus Green-Ellis RB (CIN) 8
Vernon Davis TE (SF) 9	C.J. Spiller RB (BUF) 8	Jason Witten TE (DAL) 5	Jahvid Best RB (DET) 5	Demaryius Thomas WR (DEN) 7	Marques Colston WR (NO) 6	Steve Smith WR (CAR) 6	Miles Austin WR (DAL) 5	Isaac Redman RB (PIT) 4	Kenny Britt WR (TEN) 11
Percy Harvin WR (MIN) 11	Dwayne Bowe WR (KC) 7	Eli Manning QB (NYG) 11	Jacob Tamme TE (DEN) 7	Matt Ryan QB (ATL) 7	Vincent Jackson WR (TB) 5	Tony Romo QB (DAL) 5	Robert Griffin QB (WAS) 10	Willis McGahee RB (DEN) 7	Steven Ridley RB (NE) 9
Jonathan Stewart RB (CAR) 6	Mark Ingram RB (NO) 6	LeGarrette Blount RB (TB) 5	Steve Johnson WR (BUF) 8	Antonio Brown WR (PIT) 4	Tony Gonzalez TE (ATL) 7	DeAngelo Williams RB (CAR) 6	Donald Brown RB (IND) 4	DeSean Jackson WR (PHI) 7	Jeremy Maclin WR (PHI) 7
Peyton Manning QB (DEN) 7	Brandon Lloyd WR (NE) 9	Torrey Smith WR (BAL) 9	James Starks RB (GB) 10	Michael Bush RB (CHI) 6	Peyton Hillis RB (KC) 7	Eric Decker WR (DEN) 7	Robert Meachem WR (SD) 7	Daniel Thomas RB (MIA) 7	Brandon Pettigrew TE (DET) 5
Pierre Garcon WR (WAS) 10	San Francisco Defense DEF (SF) 9	Pittsburgh Defense DEF (PIT) 4	Ryan Williams RB (ARI) 10	Baltimore Defense DEF (BAL) 9	Felix Jones RB (DAL) 5	Ben Tate RB (HOU) 8	Houston Defense DEF (HOU) 8	Ben Roethlisberger QB (PIT) 4	Philip Rivers QB (SD) 7
Reggie Wayne WR (IND) 4	Rashard Mendenhall RB (PIT) 4	Toby Gerhart RB (MIN) 11	Philadelphia Defense DEF (PHI) 7	Mikel Leshoure RB (DET) 5	Chicago Defense DEF (CHI) 6	Andy Dalton QB (CIN) 6	Isaiah Pead RB (STL) 9	David Wilson RB (NYG) 11	Sidney Rice WR (SEA) 11
Knowshon Moreno RB (DEN) 7	Fred Davis TE (WAS) 10	Denarius Moore WR (OAK) 5	Matt Flynn QB (SEA) 11	Andrew Luck QB (IND) 4	Jay Cutler QB (CHI) 6	Anquan Boldin WR (BAL) 9	Carson Palmer QB (OAK) 5	Justin Blackmon WR (JAC) 6	Matt Schaub QB (HOU) 8
Shane Vereen RB (NE) 9	Titus Young WR (DET) 5	Josh Freeman QB (TB) 5	Michael Floyd WR (ARI) 10	Malcolm Floyd WR (SD) 7	Randy Moss WR (SF) 9	Green Bay Defense DEF (GB) 10	Lance Moore WR (NO) 6	Owen Daniels TE (HOU) 8	Mike Williams RB (OAK) 5
Jermaine Gresham TE (CIN) 8	Stephen Gostkowski PK (NE) 9	Jason Hanson PK (DET) 5	Nate Kaeding PK (SD) 7	Matt Prater PK (DEN) 7	Alex Henery PK (PHI) 7	Mason Crosby PK (GB) 10	Sebastian Janikowski PK (OAK) 5	NY Jets Defense DEF (NYJ) 8	David Akers PK (SF) 9
Darrius Heyward-Bey WR (OAK) 5	Sam Bradford QB (STL) 9	Coby Fleener TE (IND) 4	Mike Williams WR (TB) 5	Santonio Holmes WR (NYJ) 9	Joe Flacco QB (BAL) 9	Jared Cook TE (TEN) 11	Santana Moss WR (WAS) 10	Robbie Gould PK (CHI) 6	Seattle Defense DEF (SEA) 11

Round

1: LeSean McCoy – **Upside outstanding. Multiple ways to beat you in PPR. Little competition for touches. Weapons on team decrease his risk. Ultimately, perhaps safest pick.**

Other Option: Ray Rice

2: Andre Johnson – **Regression rears head early. Johnson undervalued because of injury. Scarcity of pick is amazing too, as next WR drafted was Brandon Marshall (big drop). No-brainer here.**

Other Option: Matt Forte

3. Drew Brees – **Rodgers, Brady, Brees the elite QBs this year. Even with Saints controversy, Brees will be fine. He's safe and perhaps undervalued, if anything.**

Other Option: Hakeem Nicks

4. Reggie Bush – **RBs getting scarce. Bush scarcest player for me, ranked far ahead of Jahvid Best/CJ Spiller. Remember, this is PPR.**

Other Option: AJ Green

5. Mike Wallace – **Debated Witten here, but went with Wallace because value is too good. Currently upset about contract, but he has little leverage and will play opening day. Should be a No. 1 fantasy WR.**

Other Option: Jason Witten

6. Vernon Davis – **Almost got Witten anyway. Davis a drop, but not too substantial. Next TE taken was Jacob Tamme, so again, scarce player.**

Other Option: Dwayne Bowe

7. Percy Harvin – **Thought about Steve Johnson too, but Percy has more ways to score. Naturally low risk inherent to his game.**

Other Option: Steve Johnson

8. Jonathan Stewart – **Don't advocate RBs that don't catch the ball, but Stewart's rushing upside great enough to make him value here. Next best RBs on board James Starks, Felix Jones, etc.**

Other Option: James Starks

9. Peyton Manning – **The first true value selection. With Brees already on board, most would bypass Manning. Took him as trade bait. Big first few weeks, and I can get a third, fourth-round talent out of him. Okay to gamble like this late. Of course only option in re-draft leagues.**

Other Option: Torrey Smith

10. Pierre Garcon – **Just an upside pick here.**

Other Option: Mikel Leshoure

11. Reggie Wayne – **Not a typical selection of mine, but Wayne will still get targets from rookie QB. Key is health, but he has surprising upside in re-draft leagues. Risky with only three RBs, but went back-to-back WR to offset some risk of Johnson/Wallace/Harvin.**

Other Option: Rashard Mendenhall

12. Knowshon Moreno – On same team with Peyton, so I'll give him one more shot.

Other Option: Titus Young

13. Shane Vereen – Patriots backs are a crapshoot. Hearing good things about him though.

Other Option: Malcom Floyd

14. Jermaine Gresham – Thrilled to get high-upside insurance policy in 14th round.

Other Option: Jared Cook

15. Darrius Heyward-Bey – Could break out.

Other Option: Greg Little

Mock Draft #2

Round

1: Aaron Rodgers **– Safest pick in the draft. In leagues that start two quarterbacks he should be top selection, and in leagues that award six points for passing TDs, give him consideration there as well.**

Other Option: Chris Johnson

2. Jimmy Graham **– Purposely chose him to put my QB/TE theory into practice. Would have taken Gronkowski if available. Like I said, downside of Saints players being overblown.**

Other Option: Jamaal Charles

3. Greg Jennings **– Admittedly risky because pairing him with Rodgers, so downside could be big if Rodgers gets injured. Upside increased too, but general strategy is to limit risk early. Chose him anyway because he was by far scarcest player on my board.**

Other Option: Reggie Bush

4. Dez Bryant **– Upside is outstanding, risk overblown. Big risk bypassing RB in first four rounds, but VORP told me to forgo RB for scarcer receiver.**

Other Option: Miles Austin

5. Beanie Wells **– First disappointing pick. Don't like Wells in PPR, but he's safe best for good yardage with Fitzgerald and Floyd outside.**

Other Option: Shonn Greene

6. CJ Spiller – Not forced to go RB, but Spiller has nice upside in PPR. Fred Jackson aging.

Other Option: Jahvid Best

7. Mark Ingram – Ingram is falling way too far in drafts because of overreaction to poor rookie season. Scoop him up this late all day. Thrilled to have him as a third back.

Other Option: Robert Meachem

8. Torrey Smith – Poised to be #1 WR in Baltimore. Will be on a lot of my teams in 2012. Still, would like him as fourth WR, not third.

Other Option: Rashard Mendenhall

9. Mikel Leshoure – Time to take risk. Basically rookie with knowledge of offense. Off-field issues offset by Best's concussion history.

Other Option: Felix Jones

10. Santonio Holmes – Really disappointed with pick. Got impatient with limited WR depth and not much on board.

Other Option: Andy Dalton

11. Joe Flacco – Not a bad second quarterback. Underrated draft strategy to pair late-round QB and WR. If you experience injuries, you will need lots of upside. Second-string QB/WR pair gives you just that.

Other Option: Jermaine Gresham

12. Darrius Heyward-Bey – See Mock Draft #1

Other Option: Titus Young

13. Jared Cook – Improved all three all three years. Should get lots of targets.

Other Option: Greg Little

14. Cowboys D – Just going defense to show you where you should take one.

Other Option: Another defense you like

15. Rob Bironas – If you have to select a kicker, do it here.

Other Option: Any other kicker who is alive

Mock Draft #3

Round

1: Chris Johnson – **Regression selection. CJ is just outside top tier of McCoy, Rice, Foster. Would take him ahead of MJD.**

Other Option: Tom Brady

2: Andre Johnson – **Another draft with AJ because he falls too far. One of few drafts I didn't take QB in first two rounds. Debated Brees heavily.**

Other Option: Jimmy Graham

3: AJ Green – **Marshall on board, but Green represents less risk. If top-flight QB is here, take him.**

Other Option: Brandon Marshall

4. Reggie Bush – **This is a theme of my PPR drafts. At this point, he was only back left in my third tier. Vick was a major consideration, and in a different draft I may have taken him. Didn't because half of owners picking between this pick and my next already had QB. Didn't work out, but example of how game theory can really help. More useful near end of round.**

Other Option: Michael Vick

5: Tony Romo – **Vick almost fell, and it would have made my draft outstanding. Still happy with Romo, who had underrated 2011. Debated WRs here, but knew one I liked (DeSean Jackson, Miles Austin, Steve Johnson, Dwayne Bowe) would drop to sixth.**

Other Option: Steve Johnson

6: Dwayne Bowe – **Only one of the WRs I liked fell, but if I had gone with Bowe or DeSean in the fifth, I would have lost Romo and ended up with Eli or Peyton. Like Romo/Bowe combination more, obviously.**

Other Option: Peyton Manning

7: Tony Gonazalez – **Really wanted Pettigrew or Fred Davis. Not happy with Gonzalez, but couldn't keep bypassing TE because #1 material just not left. Gonzalez only option in re-draft leagues.**

Other Option: DeAngelo Williams

8: Mark Ingram – **See Mock Draft #2**

Other Option: James Starks

9: Rashard Mendenhall – **Going RB again with CJ2K and Bush being somewhat risky. Another high-upside pick here, and a good time to take a risk.**

Other Option: Ben Roethlisberger

10: Malcom Floyd – **Should see a ton of targets with Vincent Jackson out.**

Other Option: Knowson Moreno

11: Joe Flacco – **Romo is a solid #1, but he isn't elite enough to not have insurance plan. Flacco by far top player left at QB spot.**

Other Option: Shane Vereen

12: Jermaine Gresham – **Good value and upside behind risky Gonzalez.**

Other Option: Titus Young

13: Jacoby Ford – **Prefer DHB, but Ford has big play potential too.**

Other Option: Randy Moss

14: Brian Quick – **Could be #1 WR in St. Louis. Bradford set to rebound, and someone has to get looks there. Intriguing player late.**

Other Option: Greg Little

15: Lamar Miller – **Not an advocate of handcuffing RBs by any means. Simply a value pick with some upside if Bush goes down.**

Other Option: Stephen Hill

14852014R00051

Made in the USA
Charleston, SC
04 October 2012